The Dynamics of Competition

The Dynamics of Competition

Understanding India's Manufacturing Sector

K. Pushpangadan
and
N. Shanta

OXFORD
UNIVERSITY PRESS

OXFORD

UNIVERSITY PRESS

YMCA Library Building, Jai Singh Road, New Delhi 110001

Oxford University Press is a department of the University of Oxford. It furthers the University's objective of excellence in research, scholarship, and education by publishing worldwide in

Oxford New York
Auckland Cape Town Dar es Salaam Hong Kong Karachi Kuala Lumpur
Madrid Melbourne Mexico City Nairobi New Delhi Shanghai Taipei Toronto

With offices in
Argentina Austria Brazil Chile Czech Republic France Greece Guatemala
Hungary Italy Japan Poland Portugal Singapore South Korea Switzerland
Thailand Turkey Ukraine Vietnam

Oxford is a registered trade mark of Oxford University Press
in the UK and in certain other countries

Published in India by Oxford University Press, New Delhi

First published 2009

ISBN-13: 978-019806079-6
ISBN-10: 019-806079-3

Typeset in 11/13.2 in Adobe Garamond Pro
by Excellent Laser Typesetters, Pitampura, Delhi 110 034
Printed in India by Parangat Offset, New Delhi 110 020
Published by Oxford University Press
YMCA Library Building, Jai Singh Road, New Delhi 110 001

Dedicated to

Professor K.N. Raj

For whom we have a very special place in our hearts

Contents

Tables and Figures

TABLES

Figures

Foreword

Fair competition in markets, broadly defined as rivalry among firms in the industry, is crucial not only for consumer welfare, but also for innovation and growth, and for reduction of poverty. The vital importance of competition is receiving increasing attention from policy makers, and many countries have adopted competition law and formulated competition policy in the past two decades or so.

Indian policy makers recognized the importance of competition nearly four decades ago and the MRTP (monopolies and restrictive trade practices) Act, 1969, was in force until the radical reforms of early 1990s. However, under the policy regime of License Permit.

Raj in the pre-reform era, implementation of the MRTP Act was not effective. A few years ago (2003) the Government of India set up the Competition Commission of India (CCI) in accordance with the new Competition Act, 2002. A Working Group appointed by the Planning Commission in the context of the 11th Five Year Plan submitted its Report on Competition Policy 2007. Thus, at the government level, there are new initiatives to foster competition in the Indian economy.

There are only few research studies on competition in Indian manufacturing industries covering the post-liberalization period. Professors K. Pushpangadan and N. Shanta have done yeomen service to the economics profession by producing the present study, *The Dynamics of Competition: Understanding India's Manufacturing Sector*. It is the fruit of several years of scholarly and assiduous research by the two authors. The focus of the study is on the dynamic aspects of competition, and its analytical framework is rooted in the Schumpeterian theory of the capitalist process.

Data on output/sales, cost of production, and product price at the firm level for all firms in narrowly defined industries producing a homogenous product is required for meaningful analysis of competition. Individual researchers do not have easy access to such data. Fortunately, for the last few years CCI has been sponsoring and funding research projects on topics of policy and advocacy relevance. The empirical analysis in the present study is based on a balanced panel data set for nearly 500 companies for the years 1988–9 to 2000–1. CMIE's data set PROWESS is the basic data source. The sample companies were classified into 14 industry groups and the analysis was conducted at the industry group level. The study covers four important aspects of competition: inter-temporal mobility of firms, static and dynamic aspects of concentration, persistence of profit rates, and impact of domestic competition on trade performance.

For the analysis of mobility, a modified turnover index has been devised through an order preserving transformation of the basic data. The mobility has been found to be very low in several industry groups with a combined share of about 70 per cent in the total net value added of the sample firms; implying a low degree of competition. The analysis of the movement of market shares among firms in Chapter 3 shows that during the sub-period 1995–2001, the Herfindahl index increased for 10 out of 14 industry groups. To access dynamic competition, Mueller's methodology involving the estimation of an autoregressive profit equation has been estimated. The empirical results in Chapter 5 demonstrated that domestic competition affects trade performance; a strong relationship between speed of adjustments of profit rate and export growth. However, increasing imports have not led to reduction in cost.

The literature dealing with the assessment of competition in the Indian manufacturing sector is quite limited. This study is comprehensive in its scope, it employs appropriate tools of analysis and comes up with new empirical findings and insights. The authors deserve unqualified compliments for accomplishing a valuable and difficult task. It is hoped that young scholars will be inspired to take up further research on important analytical and policy issues in the area of competition in the coming years.

Students and teachers of Indian industry, researchers in this area, policy analysts, and policy makers will find much valuable material in the book.

K.L. Krishna
Centre for Development Economics
Delhi School of Economics, Delhi
and
Centre for Economic and Social Studies, Hyderabad

Preface

Jointly working on this book has been a rich and satisfying experience. What began initially is an attempt to write a joint paper, through constant interaction, exchange of ideas and thoughts, and wide reading crystallized into this book. Each of the chapters has been vetted through seminar presentations and classroom teaching both within India and abroad. We are particularly grateful to Professor V.N. Balasubramanyam of Lancaster University and Dr T.G. Arun of Manchester University for facilitating the presentations in UK. Over and above these we have had the privilege of receiving valuable comments from renowned scholars like Professors K.K. Subrahmanian, D.U. Sastry, and other unknown referees of our papers published in different reputed journals. All this has helped to improve, add clarity, and provide rigour to chapters within the book. We are grateful to all of them. We would like to specially acknowledge our gratitude to the editors of *Economic and Political Weekly* (EPW), ICFAI *Journal of Industrial Economics and Indian Economic Review* for granting us permission to include articles, which initially appeared in their journals, in this book. More specifically Chapter 2 is a modified version of a paper titled 'Competition in Indian Manufacturing Industries: A Mobility Analysis' (EPW, No. XLI, 30 September 2006). Chapter 3 is a revised version of a paper titled, 'Competition in Indian Manufacturing Industries: A Study using Static and Dynamic Measures of Concentration' (ICFAI *Journal of Industrial Economics*, Vol. 2, No. 1, 2005); and Chapter 4 is a revised version of the paper titled 'Competition and Profitability in Indian Manufacturing Industries' (*Indian Economic Review*, Vol. 43, No. 1, 2008). Closer home we have benefited from the constructive comments of our colleagues, Professors P. Mohanan Pillai, P. Sivanandan, U.S. Mishra, Sunil

Mani, K.J. Joseph, N. Vijayamohanan Pillai, K. Navaneetham, P.L. Beena, M. Parameswaran, and G. Murugan from the Bureau of Economics and Statistics, Government of Kerala. We are deeply indebted to all of them. The constant support and encouragement of Professors Pillai, Sivanandan, Pulapre Balakrishnan, and Murugan in this endeavour deserves special mention.

We will be failing in our duty if we do not place on record our deep gratitude to Professor K.L. Krishna. He took immense interest in our work and patiently went through our various drafts. In the midst of his several preoccupations and tight schedules, he always found time for us. This work has gained much from his valuable suggestions. Most importantly he agreed to our request to write a foreword to this book. We are very much honoured and thankful to him in this regard.

We also place on record the support of Professor K. Narayanan Nair, Director, Centre for Development Studies for all his help in this venture. There are several others at the Centre whose support has been very valuable, and to whom we are obliged, but constraints of space restrain us from listing their names. Special mention, however, needs to be made of the unstinted help and cooperation of Sri Anil Kumar, Information and Documentation Officer, Centre for Development Studies, for getting us all the relevant literature, even the ones difficult to access. But for him we would have been much poorer in our reading. Our heartfelt gratitude to him. We also thank the other members of the library and the administration, who lent their helping hand whenever we needed it. Again, mention must be made particularly of V. Jayachandran, M.A. Cencymon, K. Sunil, and Sony Paul for their valuable research assistance at different stages in the preparation of this book.

We fondly dedicate this book to Professor K.N. Raj, founding father of Centre for Development Studies. Words cannot express what we owe him for having given us this wonderful institute where we began our careers, grew and matured, both as professionals and individuals. He was one who always stood for academic excellence, and we would be sufficiently rewarded if this book gets recognized as at least a small step in that direction.

There have been spin-offs from this work by way of students picking up issues and methods from this study. We hope this book provides the stimulus and inspiration for further research in this area and related fields. The usual caveats however remain.

May 2009

K. PUSHPANGADAN
N. SHANTA

Abbreviations

ASI	Annual Survey of Industries
AIC	Akaike Information Criterion
ARMA	Auto-Regressive Moving Average
CMIE	Centre for Monitoring Indian Economy
CSO	Central Statistical Organization
CV	Coefficient of Variation
DFFC	Dominant-Firm-with-Fringe Competition
DW	Durbin-Watson
FDI	foreign direct investment
FERA	Foreign Exchange Regulation Act
HI	Herfindahl Index
HP	Hymer and Pashigian
IMD	Institute for Management Development
IPR	Indian Policy Resolutions
ISI	Ijiri–Simon Index
MIC	Monopolies Inquiry Commission
MRTP	Monopolies and Restrictive Trade Practices
NTP	Net Trade Performance
OLS	Ordinary Least Square
PPI	Persistence of Profit Index
PPR	Permanent Profit Rates
R&D	Research and Development
SA	Speed of Adjustment
SBC	Schwartz Bayesian Criteria
SCP	Structure, Conduct, Performance
SSI	Small-Scale Industries
SD	Static & Dynamic
TI	Trade Involvement
TM	Transition Matrix
WTO	World Trade Organization

1

Introduction

THE BACKGROUND

Creating a competitive environment in the domestic economy has become the major policy thrust of nations that have either liberalized their economies or are in the process of doing so. The world economy as a whole has also been under increasing pressure to become competitive, with the establishment of the World Trade Organization (WTO) in the nineties (1995) and the majority of nations becoming its members. The importance of growing significance attached to competition today[1] is also clearly evident from the now common practice in the international literature of ranking countries according to their competitiveness.[2] The ranking in the World Competitiveness Report is a major criterion by which national performance is judged (Krugman 1996). Favourable rankings are also used to promote inward investment (Lall 2001).

The widespread discussion of competitiveness among business leaders, politicians, and intellectuals tends to suggest that it has an accepted definition (and measure) based on theoretical foundations. A review of the literature suggests that this is not true. The concept has its origin 'from business school literature, where it forms the

[1] The concern with competition and its measurement world over is clearly indicated in Lall (2001).

[2] The World Economic Forum which hosts the famous Davos Conferences began issuing its annual World Competitiveness Report since 1980 (Krugman, 1996). A second important index is the one prepared by the International Institute for Management Development (IMD) in the World Competitiveness Report (Lall, 2001).

basis for a great deal of strategic analysis' (Lall 2001). To Krugman it means: 'that nations compete for world markets in the same way that corporations do, that a nation which fails to match other nations in productivity or technology will face the same kind of crisis as a company that cannot match the costs or products of its rivals' (Krugman 1996, p. 17).

Economists use the term 'competitiveness' in different ways: (i) it is a measure of relative price and/or cost indices expressed in some common currency; (ii) others focus on structural factors such as productivity, innovation, skills, etc. that influence long-term performance; and (iii) some others measure it in terms of economic growth. Among the three, the first index alone treats countries as 'competing directly with each other' (Lall 2001, p. 1503).

In theory, under several strong and unrealistic assumptions, free trade is expected to optimize resource allocation. When these assumptions do not prevail, markets cannot allocate resources optimally (market failures). In these circumstances, countries may help firms to compete more effectively by following a set of macro policies for creating an enabling environment (Mehta 2006, 2007). This is particularly valid in the case of imperfect markets. The major imperfections are scale economies, increasing returns, externalities and linkages, technological leads and lags, cumulative learning, and first mover advantages. According to Lall (2001), such imperfections are particularly common in technology and innovation, the main drivers of national competitiveness.

Competitive strategy assumes importance here, which helps countries build dynamic comparative advantage. In this context the strategy for developing countries is to create new factors, markets and institutions, and capabilities that take them on to a higher growth path (Lall 2001). The European Union paper (1993)[3] on competitiveness emphasizes the need for ensuring fair competition in the market as an essential ingredient for enhancement and maintenance of competitiveness in the economy. It may be emphasized that competition per se does not ensure fair and efficient markets unless it is accompanied by competition policy (Mehta 2007).

[3] The European Union (EU) published a white paper in 1993 (cited in Mehta (2007), end note 2; p. 21.

Hence the relevance of competition policy and its significant role in promoting and ensuring fair competitiveness and growth.

Recognizing the importance of the policy framework, more than 105 countries have also passed Competition laws designed to encourage and facilitate a competitive environment and to prevent the abuse of market power. Thus, both domestically and globally, competition has become an important force to reckon with.[4] Notwithstanding this, there are several unsettled theoretical and empirical issues relating to competition. To quote Lall (2001), 'while competitiveness indices have become significant in the policy discourse in many developing countries, surprisingly little is known about their economic foundations: how soundly they are based in theory and constructed in practice'. He further adds that for any analysis to be analytically acceptable, it should focus on particular sectors rather than economies as a whole. All this clearly points to the fact that any meaningful analysis of competition has to be at the sectoral level and with a sound and appropriate theoretical base. Such theory-informed studies for the manufacturing sector in India and using multidimensional indicators of competition is however missing. Hence the motivations for this book entitled, *The Dynamics of Competition: Understanding India's Manufacturing Sector.*

THE INDIAN CONTEXT

Several happenings in India underline the pertinence of undertaking such a study for India. First and foremost, there has been a paradigm shift in India's development strategy from a controlled economy to a market economy. The primary objective of the new strategy is to open up the economy to both domestic and international competition. In this context, several reform measures have been introduced since the mid-eighties, culminating in the wider reforms of 1991, for speeding up and intensifying the process of liberalizing the domestic economy and its integration with the rest of the world. Joining the WTO has made it more imperative for India to achieve

[4] By 1990s the concept of competitiveness was no longer controversial. Competitiveness was the key, the only question was how to achieve it (Krugman 1996).

these objectives in a globalized world. Many of the provisions of the existing WTO agreements do touch on competition issues either directly or indirectly.[5] It is important to note that several of the reform measures were aimed either at transforming the manufacturing sector or had implications for it. To mention a few, reducing the role of the public sector, removal of industrial licensing, product and price controls, reduction in tariffs, removal of controls on imports, encouraging foreign direct investment, etc. were some such measures (Virmani 2006). The focus of the reform measures was on giving free play to market forces and private initiative to achieve technical progress, competitiveness, and to move to a higher trajectory of growth. A significant move in this direction and a major landmark in the reforms process in India is the enactment of the Competition Act, 2002, subsequently amended in 2007, for promoting fair competition. The broad objectives of the new Act are: (i) to promote and sustain competition in markets so that the Indian market is equipped to compete with the markets world-wide; (ii) to protect the interests of the consumers; (iii) to ensure the freedom of trade; and (iv) provide for the establishment of the Competition Commission of India—a body which will advocate competition and prevent practices having an adverse effect on competition. Besides, in the context of the Eleventh Plan, steps have been initiated to develop a comprehensive competition policy,[6] which would formulate policy instruments and strategic interventions needed to generate and foster a competitive environment and to enhance competition in the domestic markets.[7] The above developments clearly underline

[5] For details of global forums and their implications for competition and regulatory issues, see GoI, Planning Commission (2007), Basant and Morris (2000), Bhattacharjea (2001).

[6] The Planning Commission constituted a Working Group on Competition Policy vide its order No. 1 and M3 (32)/2006 dated 5th June 2006. To quote the Report, 'strengthen the forces of competition in the market, both competition law and competition policy' are required. The two complement each other. Competition law prohibits and penalizes anti-competitive practices by enterprises functioning in the market, that is, it addresses market failure. The aim of competition policy is to create a framework of policies and regulations that will facilitate competitive outcomes in the market', p. 5.

[7] GoI, Planning Commission (2007), Report of the Working Group on Competition Policy. Although Competition Acts have been in force since

the fact that domestic and international competition is a major concern for India today.

COMPETITION AND THE REGULATORY FRAMEWORK

The background to the passing of the Competition Act can be traced back to the context of the economic reforms. While the proximate cause of the wider reforms of 1991 was the external debt crisis when India was almost close to default in meeting her international repayment obligations, compounded by her mounting internal debt, the macro crisis has been widely seen as a consequence of micro inefficiencies brought about by the pursuit of wrong economic policies. A detailed examination of the various policies and their implementation will throw more light on this.

Indian industry functioned within the framework specified in the various policy resolutions and the priorities laid down in the Five Year Plans. To quote Srinivasan, 'The First Five Year Plan set the overall interventionist framework of policy, and the Second Plan (1956–61) authored by Professor P.C. Mahalanobis, provided the analytical foundation for the development strategy that was pursued for the subsequent 35 years. It emphasized the development of heavy industries, import substitution across the board, and spearheaded a vast expansion of the public sector'.[8]

The broad objectives of the industrial policy specified in the various resolutions[9] were to increase production and productivity, particularly in the priority sectors, encourage small scale industries in the interests of employment, work towards regional balance in industrial development, control foreign investment in domestic industry, and most importantly to prevent concentration of economic power by the control of monopolies and large houses.[10] The Industries Act 1951 gave legal sanction for the implementation

---

as early as 1889 (Canada), comprehensive competition policies are of more recent origin. Australia was the first to adopt a broad-based formal policy in 1995.

[8] Srinivasan (2000), pp. 2–3.

[9] For details, see Resolutions of 1948, 1956, and 1973, and the Policy statements of 1973, 1977, and 1980. See *http://www.dipp.nic.in* (Ministry of Commerce & Industry).

[10] Ahluwalia (1985).

of the policies. The expansion of the public sector was achieved through reservation of sectors for investment, nationalization of industries, financial institutions, and by controlling private activity.[11] This resulted in the setting up of a number of public monopolies with several privileges with regard to finance, imports, etc.[12] As for the private sector, through physical controls, and target setting in the five year plans, 'the system was operated in a manner calculated to influence and determine (i) the pattern of investment down to the *product*-level, and (ii) the choice of technology, extending to scale, expansions, location, direct import content, and the terms of foreign collaboration in finance and know-how'.

The most important policy instruments used for achieving the stated objectives were the Industrial licensing Policy, the import licensing policy, and other trade policies. In addition to this, there were controls on price and distribution. The aim of industrial licensing was to direct resources into socially desired directions and imposed controls both on entry and capacity expansion. It was also used to bring about regional dispersal. Several tax and other concessions were granted to encourage backward-area industrialization. All imports were subject to licensing. The aim of the import licensing policy was to provide protection to the domestic industry from foreign competition and to conserve scarce foreign exchange. In addition to this, tariffs gave further protection to domestic industry from foreign competition. As for the controls on foreign investment and import of technology, direct purchase of technology was more favoured and equity participation to be

[11] For details, see Virmani (2006), pp. 5–6. The role of the public sector was clearly defined in the Industrial Policy Resolution (IPR) of 1948. It divided industry into four categories: category 1, State monopoly covering 3 industries (defence, atomic energy, and railways); category 2, Mixed sector covering 6 industries (Aircraft, ship-building, telecom equipment, mineral oil, coal, iron); category 3, government control in 18 industries; and category 4, Private enterprise. The IPR of 1956 further expanded State monopoly to cover 16 industries as against the earlier 6 and industry got regrouped into three: category 1, State monopoly (schedule A) covering 17 industries; category 2, Mixed sector (schedule B), covering 12 industries; and category 3, Private enterprises. The logic and rationality for according a commanding role to the public sector, is clearly discussed in Chakravarty (1987), pp. 11–12.

[12] Virmani (2006), p. 13.

progressively reduced (kept below 40 per cent). Price controls aimed at the supply of essential commodities at reasonable prices.[13] Several labour laws such as the Industrial Disputes Act 1947, The Minimum Wages Act 1948, The Employees State Insurance Act 1948, and the Employees Provident Fund Act, 1952 were put in place.[14] In short, the industrial development of the country was intensively regulated.

By the early sixties it became clear that all was not quite well with the working of the system.[15] There were a number of limitations in the application and operation of the various controls and involved cumbersome administrative procedures and delay.[16] The Monopolies Inquiry Commission (MIC) set up to evaluate the working of the system clearly pointed out to the failure of the licensing system in addressing the major objective of the control of monopoly power. Analysing concentration in 20 industrial groups and for 100 products, MIC found that in 1964 in a large number of industries, a single undertaking was the only supplier or had to its credit a very large portion of the market.[17] With regard to country concentration, the Commission examined the industry composition of 75 groups with assets above 5 crore, the number of companies falling under each group, their holding of assets etc.[18] The proportion of the

[13] Sugar, cement, coal and steel, drugs, edible oils, etc. were some products which came under price control.

[14] Bhagwati and Desai (1970).

[15] This was evident from the various studies and reports such as the Monopolies Inquiry Commission Report (1965), Report on Industrial Planning and Licensing Policy (1967), Hazari (1966), Dutt Report (1969), Bhagwati and Desai (1970).

[16] See Srinivasan (2000), Ahluwalia (1985), and Virmani (2006) among others.

[17] MIC, p. 125. More detailed analysis of 100 consumer product groups showed that 65 per cent fell in the group of high concentration, 10 per cent in the group revealing medium concentration, 8 per cent in the low concentration group, and the remaining 17 per cent in the category with no concentration Estimated from data in the report in pp. 30–2, by Baskar (1992).

[18] Where 50 per cent or more of the equity was owned by an industrialist or his relatives, the company was said to be under his control. The holdings of a company under the control of a business house was also taken to be the holding of that house.

assets of the 75 groups to those of the corporate sector[19] was about 46.9 per cent while the proportion of the total paid up capital of these groups to that of the corporate sector came to 44.1 per cent in 1963–4. Big business was at an advantage in securing licenses for starting industries as well as for expansion of capacity and to secure foreign collaboration.

It was also observed that big business houses by putting in multiple and early applications for the same industry tended to corner a considerable amount of targeted capacity and thereby secured a dominant position in the industry. The advantage which big business had over smaller people for obtaining assistance from banks and other financial institutions and the law of patents were other factors. It was also seen that prima facie, there was a case of restrictive practices[20] being followed in some industries. Over and above this, the Commission also found evidence of concentration of economic power with monopolistic position in public sector enterprises in industries such as steel, fertilizers, etc.[21] It is these findings that prompted the Monopolies Enquiry Commission to recommend the setting up of a separate commission for controlling monopolies and restrictive trade practices.[22]

The period 1965–80 saw a further widening and deepening of controls over the private sector with several more restrictive laws and rules added on. The passing of the Monopolies and Restrictive Trade Practices (MRTP) Act 1969 to control and check the expansion of large industrial houses, expanding the list of SSI-reserved industries and extension of SSI reservation in1967–8 to the modern small scale industry sector, the passing of the Foreign Exchange Regulation Act (FERA) of 1973, the law relating to retrenchment of workers (1978–9), were some of the regulations

[19] Non-banking, non-governmental corporate sector.

[20] That is preventing competition, price fixation, exclusive dealership, hoarding at the time of scarcity, output restriction, etc.

[21] MIC (1965), p. 185.

[22] This was accepted by the government and the MRTP Act was passed. The findings of this Committee also resulted in the appointment of the Industrial Licensing Policy Inquiry Committee (1967) by the Ministry of Industrial Development to enquire into the workings of the licensing system during the period 1956–66.

introduced during this period. Some socialist measures were also brought in. For instance, the nationalization of banks, insurance and other related measures led to control over investment funds for the private sector. Industries such as coal, steel, and copper, etc. were also nationalized. Private initiative and competition thus came to be completely curtailed.[23]

The MRTP Act, however, failed to reduce the concentration of monopoly power and involved protracted proceedings. The scale of output was restricted in the case of MRTP companies as well. Similarly, the protection and the financial and fiscal concessions offered to small scale industries tended to prohibit industry from seeking gains from economies of scale, marketing, etc. Again there were barriers to exit of inefficient units which subsequently were treated as sick units and transferred to government. This policy tended to encourage inefficiency of entrepreneurs and they getting away with it. The policy for balanced regional development tended to lead to the fragmentation of units in the place of development of large units with economies of scale. The manner of implementation of price controls varied across industries and they also had their deleterious effects on the growth of the industry.

India's economic policy based on controls over the private sector and an inward looking trade and foreign investment strategy and a dominant public sector were, thus, the main elements that stifled efficiency.[24] According to Bhagwati,[25] 'the deadly combination of industrial licensing and controls at home with import and exchange controls externally, effectively cut off the rigour of competition from all sources and made the creation of a rentier, as against an entrepreneurial economy more likely. X- inefficiency was certain to follow'.

Srinivasan[26] sums up the working of the industrial strategy of the pre-liberalization period as follows: 'by and large the public sector has acted as a brake on private sector development. The

[23] The wide discretionary powers wielded by the bureaucrats in the implementation of the policies earned for this period the name 'license–permit quota raj'.

[24] Bhagwati and Desai (1970), p. 231.

[25] Bhagwati (1993), p. 60.

[26] Srinivasan (2000), pp. 5–6.

choice of location, technology, employment, and pricing policies of the public sector have become, and continue to be politicized so that efficient development was precluded. Far from generating resources, the public sector had become a monumental waste and liability for taxpayers. It is true that the industrialization strategy did generate a diversified industrial base and a capability for designing and fabricating industrial plants and machinery. But the strategy virtually ignored considerations of scale economies, vastly restricted domestic and import competition, constrained technological upgrading through licensing and purchase of foreign technologies, encouraged capital-intensive production, and discouraged employment generation that was further constrained by the high cost of hiring and firing imposed by our restrictive labour laws. In addition there was very little flexibility of redeploying labour even within enterprises. The consequence was a high cost and globally uncompetitive sector which was also out of tune with India's capital scarcity and labour abundance.'

The Working Group on Competition Policy[27] (GoI 2007) observed, 'the complex network of controls and regulations fettered the freedom of enterprises. Administrative delays and rent-seeking opportunities spawned an inefficient industrial structure, which was beset with problems of sub optimal scales of operation, capacity underutilization, lack of technological upgradation, and high levels of industry concentration'. Thus Indian industry, in short, was characterized by outdated technology, low productivity, high cost, and poor product quality. Licensing and capacity allocations determined number of firms and market shares respectively. In industries in which tight controls on these were exercised, concentration grew. At the other end indiscriminate grant of licenses also bred production inefficiencies. Preference for the small-scale sector gave rise to artificially low levels of concentration as well. In short, government policy shaped market structure.[28]

Although towards the late 1970s there were intense debates on the regime of controls and since the 1980s, it was becoming evident that the country was heading towards a debt crisis and a change

[27] GoI (2007), See the Working Group on Competition Policy for details.
[28] See Athreya and Kapur (2006) for more details.

in policies was urgent, political and other considerations weighed heavily against a headlong plunge. There was official retrospection (reflection) on the working of the system of controls and a number of committees were set up to examine specific issues and recommend necessary changes in Policy.[29] The findings of these committees led to the initiation of changes in the policy orientation.[30] A shift in strategy was visible in the Industrial policy statement of 1980 with its emphasis on promoting domestic competition, technological upgradation, and modernization.[31] Reforms of the eighties have however been characterized as reforms by stealth.[32] The focus of these measures was to address the distortions arising from controls on domestic production and investment and external trade. Starting in 1980–1, there was a gradual liberalization of controls on prices, production, distribution, and investment.[33] Capital market reforms were also initiated. More important were the external reforms wherein the move was from import substitution to export promotion. Some measures to liberalize imports were also undertaken.

The recognition of the drawbacks of the earlier policies and the gains from going for market reforms brought into focus the need to enhance productivity, private investment and growth, and to remove restrictions on competition in product markets and access to capital and technology. Although mid-eighties saw the beginnings of some progressive deregulation,[34] it was the macro crisis of

[29] Important among them are the Committees headed by Alexander (GoI 1978), Dagli (GoI 1979), Tandon (GoI 1980), Pande (GoI 1980) and Rajadhyaksh (GoI 1980), and most importantly the Narasimham Committee (GoI 1986) among others.

[30] Though a few reform measures were undertaken before the eighties, mostly ad hoc in nature, Panagariya (2008), Virmani (2006), among others.

[31] The reforms of the eighties were driven by necessity (slow export and manufacturing growth) pragmatism (trial and error, incremental change), personal observation of market economies, and business drive, Virmani (2006), p. 21.

[32] Since there was no official resolution or statement about the 'new economic policy' wherein 'certain changes in policy were initiated in stages' (Virmani 2006), p. 22.

[33] For details of the various measures see Virmani (2006), pp. 23–4.

[34] Virmani (2006), pp. 71–2.

1991, and the Washington consensus whose principal components are privatization, liberalization, and globalization that precipitated matters.

To quote Bhagwati and Srinivasan,[35] 'the macro economic crisis thus provided the opportunity and the necessity finally to address meaningfully the inefficiencies in our policy framework that had hurt our economic performance and to begin seriously the task of undertaking the necessary micro-economic or structural reforms as well. These reforms necessitating an exhaustive restructuring of our policy framework had become critically necessary'. The objective was to move from an inefficient to an efficient economy, increase growth and reduce poverty.

The Industrial policy statement of 1991 emphasized technological dynamism and international competitiveness.[36] This was achieved by liberalization of industry, trade, and the external sector. In the case of industry, all licensing requirements were abolished and the areas reserved for the public sector reduced, including the number of products reserved for the small-scale sector. All quantitative restrictions of imports were removed, foreign direct investment (FDI) was liberalized, and the rupee was made partly convertible on trade account. The focus was on freeing the economy from controls and allowing full play of the market forces to promote both domestic and international competition. With a view to meet the new challenges, India replaced the earlier MRTP Act (1969) with the Competition Act, 2002. In contrast to the old Act with its focus on restricting monopolies, the new Act focuses on promoting fair competition. Today along with monetary, fiscal, and trade policies, competition policy has become a critical component of overall economic policy.[37] The paradigm shift in policy had completed the full circle and competition has come to stay. This takes us to the theoretical perspectives on competition.

[35] Bhagwati and Srinivasan (1993), p. 4.

[36] GoI, Planning Commission (2007), *Report of the Working Group on Competition Policy*.

[37] See for details, GoI (2000), *Report of the High Level Committee on Competition Policy and Law*.

THE THEORETICAL PERSPECTIVE[38]

There is no exact definition of competition but different notions of competition exist in the literature. Let us cite a few important ones here. According to McNulty (1967, 1968), the most accepted notion of competition was to consider it as the opposite of monopoly. Stigler (1987) describes competition as a 'rivalry between individuals (or group or nations) and it arises when two or more parties strive for something that all cannot obtain'. According to Hayek, a concept of economic competition, if it is to be significant for economic policy, 'ought to relate to patterns of business behaviour such as might reasonably be associated with the verb' 'to compete' (McNulty 1968). Notwithstanding these various definitions, two dominant strands of thought emerge from the literature: one, which treats competition as a state of affairs, and the other, treats it as a process. The first one is static and the second one is dynamic in nature. For a proper understanding of these two views, they need to be placed in the historical context of their evolution.

Generally three great names are associated with that of competition: Adam Smith, Cournot, and Edgeworth. We begin with Adam Smith, the father of modern economics and the prominent among classical economists. His concept of competition as expounded in his *Wealth of Nations* was one of rivalry between buyers and sellers, which would force price to a level where supply and demand would be in equilibrium. By extending the logic to all the sectors of the economy, he could provide a theory of resource allocation in the economy. To be more precise, through competition, resources move to sectors where returns are rare and prices to the lowest level. Hence, his view of competition is an ordering force in the allocation of resources in an efficient way, the dominant view of the classical economics.[39] It may be noted that his concern was with the level

[38] We have drawn much from the works of McNulty (1967, 1968), Stigler (1957, 1987), Blaug (1997), and Vickers (1995) in writing this section.

[39] McNulty (1967) argued that by the time Adam Smith's 'Wealth of Nations' appeared, the concept of competition was very familiar in economic writings such as in that of Cantillon, Turgot, Hume, and Stuart among others and its role was to bring market prices to a level where there will be no excess

of prices and not with market models of monopoly or competition. He is more concerned with the regulation of prices resulting from the presence or absence of competition. No doubt he did acknowledge that a larger number of competitors would make competition more effective as a price-determining force, but did not identify competition with a particular market structure. With the 'Wealth of Nations', price determination through the principle of competition replaced the 'earlier ethically and politically oriented price administration as the focus of economic analysis' (McNulty 1967, p. 396).

But the concept of competition (perfect) employed by nineteenth century economists was not the same as that of Adam Smith. The refinement of this concept started by Cournot, 'continued through the works of Jevons, Edgeworth, and J.B. Clark, reaching its fullest expression in Frank Knight' (McNulty 1967, p. 397), culminated in a basic conceptual change. In this analytical construct, price became a parameter to the firm rather than a variable. According to Stigler (1957), 'the mathematical economists defined competition as that situation in which *P* (price) does not vary with *Q* (quantity), in which the demand curve facing the firm is horizontal'. This is drastically different from Smith's concept for whom competition meant nothing but the necessity for the individual seller or buyer to raise or lower the price or offer in response to market conditions (McNulty 1967). The fundamental difference between Smith and the mathematical economists, however, is that Smith did not conceive of competition as 'a situation' at all, but rather as an active process leading to a certain predicted result through which the equation of price and cost was achieved. More importantly, Smith was not unaware of the presence of organizational and technological elements in competition.[40]

---

profits. Adam Smith's contribution is stated to be the systemization of earlier thinking on the subject and more importantly to raise it to the level of a general organizing principle of economic society.

[40] McNulty (1967). McNulty in a subsequent paper (1968) says, 'Adam Smith failed to relate productive technique to competition. Although he spoke of new division of labour and new improvements of art being adopted by producers to undersell competitors, it was just a passing comment'.

Cournot's concept of competition was 'totally devoid of behavioural content' since his focus was in defining competition as rigorously as possible to understand its effect. Rather than the actual workings of competition, he was concerned with its limit when no firm could affect prices by changing his output. In other words, his concern was not competition as a process but as a state in which that process had run to its limits. But Cournot was not explicit on market structure since he paid no attention to entry and, therefore, the model applies to few sellers (Oligopoly) or large number of sellers (Stigler 1957, p. 6). It was the work of Jevons, Edgeworth, and Clark in the late nineteenth century that led to the merging of the concepts of competition and the market and which was later refined and developed fully by Frank Knight (McNulty 1968). It is from these beginnings that the standard, static perfect competition model of market structure, the concept of perfect competition as we know today evolved, and which became the criterion to judge the efficiency of actual markets. Soon the concept of competition as a process was overshadowed by an end state. By 1930s, the perfect competition model, totally replaced the concept of competition as a process with an end state (Blaug 1997).

THE PERFECT COMPETITION MODEL

The main assumptions underlying this model are: existence of a large number of buyers and sellers, homogenous output, free entry and exit, perfect information, and perfect divisibility of output. Most importantly it assumes profit maximizing behaviour with given tastes and technology. In this approach the intensity of competition as 'a state of affairs' is assessed in terms of structural characteristics such as number of firms, market shares, and other variables that describe the position of an industry at a point in time. In other words, concern is with the end result of competition among sellers and buyers and not how it reached that position.[41] Under profit maximizing behaviour, the equilibrium in the competitive market is attained by equating price with marginal cost of production. In the long run the equilibrium condition depends on the cost (supply) curve of the firm. If the average cost curve is of the standard

[41] Ibid.

U-shaped form, then in the long run, profit will be driven to a minimum level. If the size of the market is large relative to the size of the firm, then economic profit will be zero and the rates of return on investment, in turn, should equalize in all industries.

Several economists[42] questioned the assumptions underlying this model. According to Clark (1940), the assumptions of this model and its outcomes are more suited to a stationary state. The infinitely elastic supply and demand curves of perfectly competitive equilibrium seem inapplicable to periods of changing market condition. For Hayek (1948), the perfect competition model describes an equilibrium situation but says nothing about the competitive process, which led to that equilibrium. According to Schumpeter, perfect competition model speaks nothing about productive and dynamic efficiency which are more important than allocative efficiency for economic well-being. Vickers (1995) and Schumpeter (1950) insisted on the irrelevance of the concept of competition to an understanding of the capitalist process in a world characterized by innovation and adaptation, survival, and failures among firms. Besides the state of affairs approach embodied in perfect competition assumes away many aspects fundamental to business behaviour such as price war, differentiation of products, etc. There was little recognition and virtually no analysis of entrepreneurship in this approach. Kirzner (1973) emphasized the role of entrepreneurial rivalry in competition. According to Demsetz (1982) and others at Chicago school, there need not be any causality between the number of market players and competition.

The most important criticism is that this model is more suited to a stationary state and is not appropriate to conditions of economic change. This is because in a regime of economic change, new innovations, changing consumer demands, etc., the assumption of perfect knowledge need not prevail and to that extent the response to change can also be off the mark. Although these criticisms (most of them by the Austrian school who conceived of competition as a process) emphasized the irrelevance of the static framework for analysing competition in a situation of change, none of these

[42] J.M. Clark (1940), Kirzner (1973), Demsetz (1982), Hayek (1948), and Schumpeter (1950), Vickers (1995).

criticisms however helped to dispel the charm with the end-state view of competition. Several[43] stood by the concept of perfect competition since it provided the benchmark for the ideal, and a convenient analytical tool for several purposes. The basic reason for this is attributed to the rehabilitation[44] and ascendancy of the Walrasian General Equilibrium Theory strengthened by the New Welfare Economics, all associated with perfectly competitive general equilibrium. The advances in the economics of imperfect information, imperfect competition, and comparative static methods added further strength to retain competition as an end state in economics analysis (Vickers 1995). New Institutional Economics, Evolutionary Economics and Neo–Austrian Economics are finding a place signifying a renewed interest in dynamic processes.[45] Both Blaug (1997) and Vickers (1995) clearly state the urgency to develop the dynamic view of competition, it being the more realistic and meaningful one of the two views. This takes us to the proponents of the dynamic view and their concept of competition.

THE DYNAMIC VIEW

As against the static view, the dynamic view treats competition as a process, which is closer to Adam Smith's concept of competition. The main proponents of this theory are Marx,[46] Schumpeter (1950), Downie (1958), and J.M. Clark (1961). In the Austrian tradition,[47] competition is viewed as a constant, endogenously-driven process of rivalry.[48] The stress is very much on the properties of the process and not on the characteristics of the final state as in the static

[43] Stiglitz (1993), Samuelson and Nordhaus (1992), and Sloman (1994) among others. See for details Blaug (1997).

[44] By Hicks-Samuelson and others. See Blaug (1997) for details.

[45] Blaug (1997) cites several studies on these lines, for example, Nelson and Winter (1982), Penrose (1980), etc., to mention a few.

[46] See Baumol (2002), p. 4.

[47] Some of its main contributors such as Hayek, Schumpeter, Kirzner, etc. being Austrians.

[48] According to McNulty (1968), both the classicals and neoclassicals never related competition in any systematic way to the technique of production within or to the organizational form of the business firm itself and the concept was divorced from a major area or facet of economic activity, p. 645.

view. Of all the proponents of this school, perhaps the most acknowledged and one of the best expositions of the dynamic view of competition is the theory of the capitalist process as enunciated by Schumpeter.[49] According to him, competition is associated with the internal industrial efficiency and with the development of 'new technology, the new source of supply, and the new type of organization'. The entrepreneur is the central figure in this analytical construct and innovation, imitation, etc., are central to the process of competition. In other words, the dynamic process is of creative destruction.

He views competition as a process with certain characteristics, principally free entry. The crux of the Schumpeterian thesis is that innovation,[50] whether in products, processes, or marketing techniques or organizational structures, creates temporary monopolies and excess profits. This invites imitators, and the competitive process will lead to an erosion of excess profits. The speed with which this occurs would depend on the intensity of competition. In this dynamic view, the market is in a flux arising from the allocation of given resources for new products and production techniques and is in disequilibrium at any moment in time unlike the first view of equilibrium (Mueller [ed.], 1990). More precisely, the capitalistic process is 'a dynamic process involving innovation and adaptation, survival and failure; its outcome is a variety of products and prices that evolve in complex ways over time and are produced by a changing collection of firms' (Geroski and Mueller 1990).

To quote McNulty,[51] 'It is well known that the essence of industrialization and economic growth is a changing production function

[49] It is also to be noted that Schumpeter himself was influenced by the Marxian view of the capitalist process. For a discussion of this point, see Freeman (2003).

[50] According to McNulty (1968), although economic activity encompasses both production and exchange, the concept of competition of earlier writers has focused on exchange and price rather than quality, whose improvement takes place within the firm and which is associated with production (p. 646). On another occasion he also mentions that competition was not related to economic growth, p. 652.

[51] McNulty (1968), p. 654.

and the development of new products, techniques, and forms of business organization... Clearly the time has come to incorporate into the mainstream of economic theory...a concept of competition closer to that occasionally suggested by Adam Smith and strongly advocated by Schumpeter—competition associated with new division of labour, within the business firm, and in the industrial structure generally and one that is more closely allied with concepts of internal, especially technological efficiency'. In the same vein we find Blaug[52] stating that textbooks in economics should deal 'with firms that jostle for advantage by price and non-price competition, undercutting, and outbidding rivals in the marketplace by advertising outlays and promotional expenses, launching new differentiated products, new technical processes, new methods of marketing and new organizational forms...all for the sake of headstart profits that they know will soon be eroded...there is no doubt that competition is an active process of discovery, of knowledge formation and of "creative destruction"'.

To sum up, a critical examination of the main strands of thought in the theoretical literature on competition clearly shows that it is the dynamic, Schumpeterian view of competition that is the most appropriate framework for analysing competition in the Indian manufacturing sector, particularly in the context of liberalization and globalization of its economy. In periods of change as in the Indian manufacturing sector characterized by structural adjustment, tariff reductions, foreign capital inflows, import competition, and other policies with emphasis on technical change, free entry and growth, the Schumpeterian[53] framework seems the one best suited to understand the capitalist process.[54] On the empirical side measuring and assessing competition is not an easy task, competition being multidimensional in nature (Scherer 1973). For a proper understanding of the capitalist process we need to have different kinds of evidence and the reinforcing effect of them needs to be

[52] Blaug (1997), pp. 255–6.

[53] It is important to note that of late there have been studies enquiring whether a renaissance of Schumpeterian ideas has taken place. See Freeman (2003).

[54] This Schumpeterian version of the capitalist process also links through innovation the static and dynamic version of competition, Baumol (2002).

assessed. Previous research in this area further justifies such a framework of analysis for our study.

PREVIOUS RESEARCH

Most studies on competition in the manufacturing sector that exist for India have dealt with the static aspects of competition. While we do not outright reject static measures, it seems equally important to supplement them with dynamic aspects of competition as well. However, there have been very few attempts to understand competition in India in the dynamic framework and particularly for the post-liberalization period. These existing studies also have their limitations.

In this review we confine ourselves to the studies in the dynamic framework. One study, which uses this framework, is that of Bhavani and Bhanumurti,[55] which tries to assess the state of competition in the Indian manufacturing sector. This study makes a distinction between potential competition and actual competition. Potential competition is studied in relation to the rules and regulations that restrict competition. For example, it tries to assess in terms of new entry how easy it is to start a business in India. Indian tariff structure, as a means of stimulating competition is compared with that of other countries. Policies relating to foreign direct investment, small industry, labour etc., are also looked into in this context. The state of actual competition is studied in terms of entry of imports, transnational corporations and structural changes in terms of shifts in size distribution, ownership patterns, and forms of business organization over the period 1989–90 and 1997–8. Market structure is analysed in terms of concentration. The study uses firm level data available in Centre for Monitoring Indian Economy (CMIE) electronic database.

Bhavani and Bhanumurti (2007) study subscribes to the view that competition is a process and hence is in the dynamic framework but has a different focus. Its focus is on an assessment of the institutional structures in terms of its adequacy as well as its effectiveness in obtaining desired goals and is useful in its own right. But what is found missing here is that, although this study falls in the genre of process studies, a theory-informed analysis

[55] Bhavani and Bhanumurti (2007).

of the dynamics of the capital process is missing. There are a few studies[56] in this line, but they have been unidimensional in nature. In other words the analysis is confined to any one dynamic aspect underlying the capitalist—process, for example, the behaviour of profit rates (the details of these studies are discussed in Chapter 4). Here there is a failure to recognize the multidimensional nature of competition. For a proper assessment of the state of competition, different dimensions of the capitalist process need to be captured. Only a comprehensive study integrating the different dimensions can achieve this. This book is an attempt in that direction.

What is proposed in this book is to use a theory-informed framework—the Schumpeterian framework for assessing competition in the Indian manufacturing sector for the post-liberalization period, 1988–9 to 2000–1, using multidimensional dynamic indicators. The choice of the Schumpeterian framework for this analysis is because where private initiative is focused on and competition within and from outside the country is encouraged through various reform measures, it is basically the Schumpeterian tenets that would operate. Major dynamic indicators, structural and performance, suggested in the literature are used in the analysis for assessing competition.[57]

THE ANALYTICAL FRAMEWORK

As stated earlier, it is the Schumpeterian framework which will be used to assess competition in this study. It is important to note that there is no explicit model for testing this framework of the competition process.[58] What we propose to do here is to test the two main tenets of the Schumpeterian view of the competitive process:

1. It may be emphasized that entry and exit of firms are at the heart of Schumpeter's process of creative destruction. The

[56] Kambhampati (1995), Glen, et al. (2001).

[57] In the context of measuring economy-wide competition, Lall (2001) advocates the use of a few critical variables rather than pulling in everything that economics, management, strategy, and other disciplines suggest (p. 1520).

[58] According to Mueller (1990), Schumpeterian perspective remains just that a perspective on the nature of competition rather than a model of the competitive process. Nelson and Winter's (1982) work also does not constitute a formal test of the Schumpeterian model of the competitive process.

assumption here is that[59] much of what happens during the competitive process will be manifested by changes in relative firm position. Initial innovations are expected to follow entry of imitators, which in turn can lead to mobility or turnover of firms in an industry. Turnover of firms is a manifestation of the creative destruction that arises from innovation in technology or product markets and allows some firms to grow at the expense of others, etc. It is the way in which new competition in ideas, new methods, and new organizational techniques are transmitted to the structure of markets. As a result of the competitive struggle, firms will grow and/or decline as indicated by entry and exit from the different markets. Changes in size and efficiency can also occur in the process. This struggle can lead to share changes among different categories of firms as well.[60] Measuring this phenomenon throws light on the intensity of competition.[61]

2. The second important tenet of the Schumpeterian thesis is that entrepreneurs introduce new products, processes, etc., which lead to temporary monopolies and excess profits and the competitive process attracts new entrants, imitators, etc., and in due course of time excess profits will be eroded. The speed with which this takes place would depend on the intensity of competition. By measuring economic rent and how quickly it gets eroded would capture this dimension of the competitive process. That is the speed of adjustment of profits to their long-run equilibrium values has to be captured. This relates to the inter-temporal behaviour of profit rates of innovating firms within the domestic economy. To complete the assessment of competition in a global economy, competition among firms across countries also needs to be assessed. This, however, requires a different approach.

According to Blaug (1997), a firm is never subject to the constraints of exogenously specified demand and production

[59] See Baldwin (1998).

[60] It is important to note that Schumpeter's view accepts the fact that competition can prevail even when there are only few buyers or sellers.

[61] Baldwin (1998), p. 5.

functions. It is the task of the entrepreneur (the central figure in Research & Development [R&D] Schumpeter's analysis) to manipulate these constraints to create new markets, to stretch old ones, and to discover new processes by R&D expenditure etc. In other words, the entrepreneur creates competitive advantage[62] creating imperfect markets and increasing returns (arising from temporary monopolies). This forms the basis of the New Trade Theory of Krugman linking trade and industrial organization theory. This links domestic market structure and trade performance. This hypothesis can be verified by examining the relationship between domestic competition measured by multidimensional indices and growth in foreign trade in the Indian manufacturing sector. Now we move to the multidimensional indicators used in the book.

THE MULTIDIMENSIONAL INDICATORS

Three dimensions of competition process are examined in the present study. Chapter 2 uses a new turnover index to capture mobility of firms during the period of study. It is important to note that in the absence of reliable data on entry and exit of firms, our analysis is confined to incumbent firms only. In Chapter 3, static and dynamic aspects of concentration ratio are integrated to capture share-cutting behaviour of firms in different size groups. Thus, Chapters 2 and 3 empirically verify the implications of the competitive process on two crucial dimensions of structure of industries. Chapter 4 is concerned with the conduct of firms under profit maximizing assumption as an allocation mechanism of resources in the economy. It analyses the persistence of profit rates and decomposes it into its component elements (competitive rate of return, short and long-run rents) using auto profit equations. Under this conduct, the speed with which a deviation of profit rates from its permanent rate converges to its original level is taken as the degree of competition prevailing in the economy. The three dimensions of competition were then used for understanding the degree of competition in the manufacturing sector and its trade performance.

[62] This forms the basis for new trade theory of Krugman (1994) among others.

ORGANIZATION OF THE BOOK

As seen from the theoretical framework, competition as a process has important implications for structure and performance. The empirical analysis in this book therefore focuses on these two dimensions. The book is divided into six chapters: an introductory chapter, four empirical chapters, and a final chapter giving the summary and conclusions of the study. The introductory chapter discusses the theme of the book and its relevance particularly in the globalized context, the analytical framework, the organization of the study, and the database. Chapter 2 is titled 'Mobility Analysis—A New Approach' and assesses competition in terms of the mobility of firms, it being an important 'structural indicium', for understanding the dynamics of competition. To quote Baldwin (1998), 'much of what happens during the competitive process will be manifested by changes in relative firm position. Mobility measures provide a direct measure of the intensity of competition'. Nevertheless, the measure has its limitations. The thrust of Chapter 2 is therefore to devise a new mobility (turnover) index, which overcomes the limitations of the traditional turnover index, and to apply it for measuring industrial competition. Although the new turnover index takes care of the criticisms against the traditional index, it does not capture the nature or nuances of competition particularly the share mobility between large firms, between small firms, and across large and small firms. This is important because quite in contrast to the traditional theory, which associated competition with a large number of sellers and buyers, it is possible to come across situations of tough competition among few sellers, say, in an oligopoly structure. In the conventional framework where the distribution of shares across firms at a point of time is used to assess competition, the various situations cited above cannot be captured. Such nuances need to be captured to get a true picture of the nature and dynamics of competition. This forms the major theme of Chapter 3 titled, 'Concentration: An Integrated Approach to Static and Dynamic Aspects'. For this we use the Grossack model, which helps to gain such valuable insights on the vigour of competition in industries.

Structural changes must get reflected in the performance on the basis of the conduct of the firms. We assume that firms function as profit maximizers and concentrate on the impact analysis on long-run profit rates and trade performance. Chapter 4 examines 'Persistence of Profit Rates', within the Schumpeterian perspective. As against a mere convergence of profit rates tested in static models for competition, the dynamic view examines whether the competitive process erodes excess profits and how quickly this happens (speed of adjustment). The persistence of profit rates is analysed using Mueller's methodology (1990) based on auto profit equations.

Lastly, Chapter 5 titled 'From Domestic Competition to Foreign Trade Performance' assesses the impact of domestic competition on trade performance, the ultimate test of economic performance. What is attempted in this chapter is an integration of the theory of industrial organization with that of international trade emphasizing the role of competitive advantage in determining trade outcomes. This is consistent with the 'new trade theory' of Krugman (1994). Multidimensional indices of competition process are used to test whether domestic market structure influences trade performance in general and imports and exports in particular. The chapter also brings together the findings on different dimensions of competition and draws conclusions on the state of competition prevailing in the manufacturing sector. Chapter 6 gives the conclusions and policy implications.

THE DATA

The best published source available for this purpose is the data assembled by the CMIE in electronic form commonly known as Prowess[63] data. The nature of this data is such that the sample size changes every year, some firms being dropped and some being added. In other words, the database is an unbalanced panel. The reasons for this are probably non-availability of data and need not necessarily imply entry into or exit from any industry. Therefore, we cannot include entry and/or exit of firms in our analysis with this data. More importantly, to analyse mobility, share-cutting, identity change, and such other issues undertaken in the present study, one needs to work with the same cohort of firms, that is, firms that

[63] CMIE, Prowess (1997, 2001).

have existed throughout the period of study. This necessitates the use of a balanced panel of firms for the analysis. What was needed was therefore to select as large a sample both in the aggregate and industry-wise and for as long a period as possible. Applying these criteria, we have obtained a balance panel of 497 firms covering 14 industry groups for the period 1988–9 to 2000–1 for our study. Two points need to be clarified here.

First, the economic concept of industry is very clear in the case of perfectly competitive markets and monopoly. In the former case the industry is characterized by many firms producing a homogenous product. In the case of monopoly, there is only a single producer and the firm and industry are one and the same. In between these two extremes there are several imperfect market structures, characterized by with and without product differentiation. In such cases, industry grouping is identified using standard industrial classification based on main activities of the firm. In our study also the standard industrial classification of CSO is applied for classifying CMIE data on firms to various industry groups.[64]

Second, an examination of the data showed that a uniformly narrow definition of industry group was not possible because the sample size in several industries was too small for any meaningful analysis. The maximum sample size in each of the 14 industrial groups was found at the end point 2001–2 starting from 1988–9. In other words, the balanced panel of firms reaches maximum in 2001–2 and drastically declines thereafter. Therefore, we have not considered data beyond the year 2000–1 for the present analysis and the period of study is selected as 1988–9 (in short, 1988–9) to 2000–1 (in short, 2000–1), one that largely coincides with the period of reforms. The overlapping of the years indicates that data relate to financial year.

The data has several limitations however. The sample is not selected on the basis of any formal sampling procedure but is based on the availability of annual reports for at least two consecutive years and with a turnover of more than Rs 2.5 crore. As a result, it does not cover small and tiny firms in the manufacturing sector. Choudhury (2002) analyses the statistical properties of the data in

[64] See Veeramani (2001), Appendix I.

detail and brings out the limitations of using a balanced panel.[65] Since our study is mostly on explorations in methodology for measuring competition process, the data limitations are not a very serious issue. The methodology can be used for new data sets, new samples, and homogeneous groups for generating 'stylized facts' on dynamic competition in Indian manufacturing industries for policy analysis.

COVERAGE OF THE SAMPLE

By the above criterion we have 14 industrial groups covering a wide range of products as seen from Table 1.1. The coverage of the CMIE sample data is not given in the Prowess Manual (1997a). Hence, one has to relate the sample data to variables relating either to all companies in each industry or to all factories in the industry. However, information on all companies in each industry is not available. Hence, we relate our sample information to data from the Annual Survey of Industries (GoI [CSO] 1992), which relates to the entire factory sector covering corporate, non-corporate, and government units. Table 1.1 provides the details of the coverage. It is observed that the sample of 497 firms covering 14 industry groups account for 27 per cent of output, 48 per cent of fixed assets, and 33 per cent of net value added in the organized manufacturing sector in 1988–9. When we consider the industry-wise coverage, the share of output ranges from 8 per cent to 70 per cent that of fixed capital from 20 per cent to 86 per cent, and of net value added from 10 per cent to 82 per cent. It is important to note that coverage below 15 per cent is observed only in two cases: for food products in terms of output, and wood and paper in terms of net value added. The relative importance of the different industry groups in the sample can be seen from the last column which gives the share of net value added of the sample companies in each industry group to the total net value added of the 497 firms covering 14 industry groups. The relative importance of different industries varies from 2 per cent for wood and paper and metal products to 19 per cent for iron and steel.

[65] For a detailed discussion of the inadequacies of the data, see Shanta and Raja Kumar (1999) and Choudhury (2002) among others.

Table 1.1
The Sample Size by Industry Group
(1988–9/2000–1, Balanced Panel)

Industry Group	Number of firms	Percentage Share of Sample Companies in Total Manufacturing (GoI [CSO] 1992)			Share of Sample Firms in Each Industry in Total Net Value Added of 497 Firms %
		Value of Output	Fixed Capital	Net Value Added	
Beverages & Tobacco	14	26.42	49.46	25.95	4.1
Cotton Textiles	51	21.69	24.74	24.00	4.0
Drugs & Pharmaceuticals	30	45.65	33.34	42.38	4.7
Electrical Machinery	47	44.71	50.17	46.24	12.4
Electronics*	30				
Food Products	41	7.73	20.86	16.16	5.0
Iron & Steel	25	53.93	86.00	66.84	18.8
Metal Products	22	27.12	24.86	23.54	2.0
Non-electrical Machinery	59	69.94	70.70	82.48	13.0
Non-ferrous Metals **	16	58.93	197.58	79.15	8.0
Non-metallic Minerals	48	52.76	67.07	44.41	6.1
Synthetic Textiles	22	26.11	51.48	40.14	2.2
Transport Equipment	72	69.67	74.50	68.18	18.0
Wood & Paper	20	15.69	35.51	10.26	1.9
All Industries	497	38.77	55.39	46.49	100

Source: CMIE, Prowess (2005), GoI [CSO] (1992).
Notes: * Since an appropriate concordance of industrial grouping between CMIE and Annual Survey of Industries could not be obtained for this group, it is included under Electrical machinery.

** The share of fixed assets is higher than 100 per cent for this industry. This may be because some large firms included in CMIE data are not covered by CSO. Such anomalies were also observed by Veeramani (2001) as well.

2

Mobility Analysis

A New Approach

INTRODUCTION

In the literature the mobility of firms in an industry is identified as one important dimension—a dynamic one, of what constitutes effective competition.[1] According to Singh and Whittington, the study of mobility of firms in an industry by enquiring into the amount of mixing and reordering that takes place in the size ranks of individual firms, focuses on the dynamic aspects of industrial structure.[2] In this context it would be useful to point out here that public policy might be concerned more with a measure of mobility or the turnover of firms in an industry, which would provide a better index of what constitutes 'equality of opportunity' rather than the usual measures of concentration.[3] In the discussions on what constitutes effective competition, Ijiri and Simon (1977) point out that a 'frequent and sizeable change in the ranks of firms in an industry would indicate vigorous competition in the industry. On the other hand, if the ranks do not change frequently, it is an indication of little competition'. On measuring the dynamics

[1] Baldwin (1998), Ijiri and Simon (1977), Boyle and Sorenson (1971), Singh and Whittington (1968), Gort, (1963), Joskow (1960), and Simon and Bonini (1958).

[2] Singh and Whittington (1968), p. 94.

[3] Ijiri and Simon (1977), p. 14.

of competition, according to Baldwin,[4] 'much of what happens during the competitive process will be manifested by changes in relative firm position. Mobility measures provide a direct measure of the intensity of competition'.

Again, the turnover measure can throw light on important dimensions of competition, which cannot be captured by the structural indices such as the concentration ratios. For instance, the *n-firm* concentration ratio can remain the same, but the identity of the firms in the group can change because of competition. This can be captured only by the turnover measure. Besides, for identifying the market structure of an industry, an understanding of the transition of firms is essential.[5] In short, given the multidimensional nature of competition[6] and the special attributes of rank analysis, it is an important 'structural indicium' for understanding competition.

This, however, does not mean that this measure has been free from controversies. One major debate in the literature is the utility of the turnover index as a measure of market behaviour. At one end you find this measure being encouraged as a useful tool for measuring competition and a replacement for concentration ratios,[7] while at the other end there were others[8] who did not consider it a useful concept for the reason that it recorded events of little economic significance and dismissed it as a useless measure.[9] Midway between the two some find it a useful supplement and additional indicia for understanding competition.[10]

Our critical review of the literature has led to the conclusion that if the limitations of the turnover index are taken care of, it can provide several important insights on competition, which cannot

[4] Baldwin (1998). He, however, adds that there can be instances when there is intense competition between firms with no change in relative position. He treats such instances as exceptions, and adds that it is unlikely that there are a large number of intense struggles occurring in which no winner emerges, p. 4.

[5] For an illustration, see Pushpangadan and Shanta (2004).

[6] Scherer (1973).

[7] Joskow (1960), Simon and Bonini (1958), Hart and Prais (1956).

[8] Hymer and Pashigian (1962).

[9] Ibid.

[10] Joskow (1960), Simon and Bonini (1958).

be captured by other indicators and is, therefore, an important tool for analysing competition.

The objective of this chapter is, therefore, to devise an improved turnover index, which overcomes the limitations of the traditional turnover index, and to apply it for measuring industrial competition. More specifically, using the new method, this chapter examines the mobility of firms in the Indian manufacturing sector for the post-reform period.

Towards this end, the specific objectives of this chapter are the following:

1. Critically examine the turnover index and provide an alternative;
2. Using the new index, test the stability of size ranks and analyse the changes in the degree of mobility;
3. Study the change in size distributions of industries and their inter- and intra-class mobility; and
4. Test for the relationship between the dynamic index of competition and the direction of mobility of firms among manufacturing industries.

This chapter is organized into 5 sections. Section 1 gives the scope and objectives and Section 2, the data and concepts used. Section 3 examines the main criticisms against the traditional turnover index and provides an alternative. Section 4 gives the empirical results based on the new turnover index followed by the summary and conclusions in Section 5.

DATA AND MEASUREMENT OF VARIABLES

The entire analysis is based on data from CMIE (Prowess), details of which have already been explained in Chapter 1.

Measurement of Size

In the literature various measures of size such as net value added, sales, total assets, and employment are used and the problems associated with them are discussed in detail[11] and there is no

[11] Sutton (1997), Curry and George (1983), and Shalit and Sankar (1977).

agreement on the best measure of size. In this situation we have selected the appropriate size variable based on a correlation analysis amongst the three commonly used measures for which we have data.

Correlation coefficients between three possible measures of size (sales, total net assets, and net value added) have been computed for 14 industrial groups at the beginning of the period, 1988–9, and at the end of the period, 2000–1, and the results are reported in Table 2.1. It is interesting to note that all are highly correlated except for one or two industries for both the years. Since the correlation coefficients between all the three measures are quite high and significant for almost all the industries, the three measures can be interchangeably used. In our analysis, we use total net assets as the measure of size.

Table 2.1
Correlation Coefficients of Alternative Pairs of Measures of Size by Industry Group 1988–9 and 2000–1

Industry Group	1988–9			2000–1		
	Sales/ Net Value Added	Sales/ Total Net Asset	Net Value Added/ Total Net Asset	Sales/ Net Value Added	Sales/ Total Net Asset	Net Value Added/ Total Net Asset
Beverage & Tobacco	0.93	0.87	0.96	0.99	1.00	0.99
Cotton Textiles	0.89	0.12	0.42	0.52	0.31	0.92
Drugs & Pharmaceuticals	0.96	0.89	0.87	0.97	0.92	0.88
Electrical Machinery	0.97	0.95	0.94	0.85	0.96	0.82
Electronics	0.92	0.88	0.98	0.83	0.88	0.78
Food Products	0.86	0.74	0.81	0.69	0.73	0.84
Iron & Steel	0.99	0.88	0.87	0.98	0.97	0.92
Metal Products	0.96	0.92	0.91	0.92	0.88	0.90
Non-electrical Machinery	0.99	0.98	0.99	0.99	0.99	0.99
Non-ferrous Metals	0.88	0.60	0.58	0.91	0.95	0.96
Non-metallic Minerals	0.93	0.93	0.77	0.90	0.92	0.94
Synthetic Textiles	0.95	0.94	0.84	0.24	0.88	0.44
Transport Equipment	0.96	0.82	0.83	0.68	0.90	0.70
Wood & Paper	0.73	0.56	–0.07	0.97	0.96	0.92

Sources: CMIE, Prowess, (2005), GoI [CSO] (1992).

THE NEW TURNOVER INDEX

Although several limitations of the turnover index have been raised in the literature, we focus our analysis on the two major criticisms, most relevant to the measurement of competition, raised by Hymer and Pashigian (1962). The first relates to the rank ordering by size and the second to the relationship between turnover and market behaviour. The main drawback of rank ordering of size, is that it shows only whether the size of a firm is larger or smaller than that of another firm but not by how much. This is a serious problem in a rank-shift analysis. Hymer and Pashigian, using the example of the shoe industry from Joskow's paper, convincingly argue this point.

To quote Hymer and Pashigian, 'At the top of the industry, a difference of rank is large absolutely and relatively; some substantial force is needed to close the gap. But the great bulk (say seven-eighths) of the rank differences in Joskow's sample are trifling absolutely and relatively, and so are changes in rank.'[12] Such rank changes signify nothing. In other words, while there is almost no competition, such rank shifts signify otherwise.

The second major criticism is that the changes in market shares, which is the really significant phenomenon for understanding the market, does not get reflected in the rank analysis. Hymer and Pashigian graphically illustrate this by examining these changes and ranks of two leading firms, Ford and General Motors, from the US automobile industry.[13] They show that even when there were large changes in market shares, there were no changes in ranks.

In short, the main argument against the use of rank correlation to understand competition is that it does not take into account size variations. That is, it is based on rank-ordered data derived only from the order of the numbers and not the difference between them. Such ordinal measures provide information regarding greater than or less than status, but not how much greater or less. This problem is overcome by normalizing the data through an order preserving transformation as detailed below.

Let there be *n* firms in an industry and $S_1 \ldots S_n$ represent their sizes in the ascending order of magnitude. To get the order

[12] Hymer and Pashigian (1962), p. 83.

[13] Ibid.

preserving ranks incorporating the size differences, the following transformation is undertaken.

$$Z_j = [S_j - \min (S_{1,} ..., S_n)]/[\max (S_1,..., S_n) - \min (S_{1,} ..., S_n)] \quad j=1, ..., n. \qquad (2.1)$$

where *min* refers to the minimum value and *max* to the maximum value of shares of *n* firms.

Equation (2.1) transforms size of firms ($S_1 \ldots S_n$) to ($Z_1 \ldots Z_n$) where the values range from 0 to 1. In order to replace the zero in this transformation, we have cumulated the series by adding the differences between two consecutive values of Z and obtain the new series on size of firms ($\bar{Z}, \ldots, \bar{Z}n$). The same procedure can be repeated for any year and the paired values of the new series for any two years can then be used for the calculation of rank correlation coefficient.

We further proceed to establish that the order preserving transformation is also related to the market shares of firms. It may be noted that Z_j is related to the share of firm j as shown below.

Dividing the numerator and the denominator in equation (2.1) by $\sum_{i=1}^{n} S_i$

$$Z_j = \frac{S_j/\sum S_i - \min(S)/\sum S_i}{\max(S)/\sum S_i - \min(S)/\sum S_i}$$

$$= \frac{S_j/\sum S_i}{\max(S)/\sum S_i - \min(S)/\sum S_i} - \frac{\min(S)/\sum S_i}{\max(S)/\sum S_i - \min(S)/\sum S_i}$$

$$= a\, Mj\text{-}b \qquad (2.2)$$

where $M_j = S_j/\sum S_i \quad j = 1, .., n$

a and b are constants.

min (S) = min ($S_{1,} ..., S_n$)

max (S) = max ($S_{1,} ..., S_n$)

Equation (2.2) clearly shows that the transformed variable Z_j of the firm j is linearly related to its market share of assets. The relationship between the new turnover measure and the market share instability index as formulated by Hymer and Pashigian[14] (HP) is tested. The HP Instability Index is defined as,

$$I = \sum_{i=1}^{n} \sum_{t=1}^{T} \left| \frac{a_{t,i}}{\bar{A}_t} - \frac{a_t - 1.i}{\bar{A}_t - 1.i} \right|$$

where

t = 1988–9, …, 2000–1,

$a_{t,i}$ = the assets of the firm *i* at time *t*,

$\bar{A}_t$ = total industry assets of time *t*,

n = number of firms, and

m = number of years.

The index *I* is obtained as follows:

For each firm, the change in the shares of total assets is first calculated for the period 1988–9 to 2000–1. The absolute value is summed up for all the firms to obtain the industry level index.

The relationship between the new turnover measure and the HP Index has been empirically verified for Indian industries and found to be statistically significant. (See Appendix to chapter 2 for details). This clearly establishes that the new measure also reflects the changes in market shares. The superiority of this measure over market shares will be established in the empirical analysis that follows. We now move to the application of the new turnover index to our data for Indian industries.

EMPIRICAL RESULTS

Having devised a new turnover index, we have undertaken three major exercises to get insight into the firms' dynamics and the nature of competition: (i) using rank correlation we test for the stability of size ranks; (ii) we estimate standard deviation of relative ranks using Ijiri–Simon method for the end points to understand the change in the degree of competition; and (iii) following Hart and Prais[15] and Singh and Whittington,[16] an analysis of the change in size structure and mobility patterns is attempted using transition matrices.

[14] Hymer and Pashigian (1962), p. 85.

[15] Hart and Prais (1956).

[16] Singh and Whittington (1968).

Stability of Size Ranks

To test for stability of size ranks, rank correlation is used. If the rank correlation between size of firms at two different points of time is not significantly different from zero, then there are frequent and sizeable changes in ranks indicating competition among the firms. On the other hand, if the correlation is significant, it implies lack of competition. There is absolutely no competition if the value of correlation coefficient is unity. In reality, the correlation coefficient can take any value between the two extremes, 0 and 1. The empirical results for the sample of industries are given in Table 2.2. We have run the correlation for two end points and for a middle year (1988–9 to 1994–5) to assess if the conclusions are sensitive to the choice of the years. We discuss the results for the terminal year first and then proceed to discuss the results for the middle year.

Table 2.2
Rank Correlation of New Transformed Firm Size for Selected Years (1988–9/1994–5 and 1988–9/2000–1)

Industry Groups	Rank Correlation of Size		Terminal over middle year (%) Change
	1988–9/2000–1	1988–9/1994–5	
Beverage & Tobacco	0.98	0.99	–1.0
Cotton Textiles	0.98	0.97	1.0
Drugs & Pharmaceuticals	0.60	0.73	–17.8
Electrical Machinery	0.90	0.88	2.3
Electronics	0.51	0.82	–37.8
Food Products	0.73	0.75	–2.7
Iron & Steel	0.94	0.96	–2.1
Metal Products	0.55	0.75	–26.7
Non-electrical Machinery	0.98	0.99	–1.0
Non-ferrous Metals	0.61	0.84	–27.4
Non-metallic Minerals	0.43	0.79	-45.6
Synthetic Textiles	0.69	0.83	–16.9
Transport Equipment	0.84	0.90	–6.7
Wood & Paper	0.70	0.87	–19.5

Sources: CMIE Prowess, (2005), GoI [CSO] (1992).
Note: All the coefficients are significant at 5 per cent level.

All the coefficients are significant at 5 per cent level. More importantly they are greater than or equal to 0.90 for 5 industries out of 14 suggesting a situation of perfect or close to perfect rigidity. It is interesting to note that perfect mobility does not prevail in any industry although they exist in varying degrees. The varying degrees of mobility can be characterized as low, medium or high mobility according to the value of the correlation coefficient. For further analysis, industries with a coefficient of less than 0.50 are treated as those with high mobility, between 0.50 and 0.75 as those with medium mobility, and above 0.75 as those with low mobility. By this classification we have only one industry with high mobility (Non-metallic Minerals). In the medium category we have 7 industries—Drug & Pharmaceuticals, Electronics, Food Products, Metal Products, Non-Ferrous Metals, Synthetic Textiles, and Wood & Paper. The remaining six industries fall in the category of those with low mobility. They are Beverage & Tobacco, Cotton & Blended Textiles, Electrical Machinery, Iron & Steel, Non-electrical Machinery, and Transport Equipment. It is worrying to note, that about 43 per cent (accounting for 70 per cent of value added of the sample companies) of the industry groups are characterized by low mobility and barriers to mobility in varying degree exist in all the industries considered for the analysis.

As for the middle year correlations, all of them are significant at the 5 per cent level. Here again in five industries (same as in the terminal period), correlation coefficient is almost equal to or greater than 0.90. As far as classifying industry by high/medium/low mobility according to the earlier criterion goes, there is no high mobility industry; in the medium category you have only three industries while 11 industry groups fall in the low mobility category. In other words, this means that 79 per cent of the industry groups were characterized by low mobility in the short period.

Although a reduction in the correlation coefficient over a longer time period is expected, what is important to note is the substantial reduction (greater than 25 per cent) in the rank correlation over the terminal period in non-metallic minerals (46 per cent), electronics, (38 per cent) non-ferrous metals (27 per cent), and metal products (27 per cent), implying increasing mobility/competition in those industry groups.

However, what is important to our analysis is that one should not only test for stability of ranks and infer from it whether size structure is flexible or rigid, but it should be supplemented with information on the change in the degree of mobility over the period, that is, the average amount of shifting in the ranks during the period. This would indicate whether competition has increased/decreased in the manufacturing sector.

Ijiri and Simon[17] suggest a measure for this—a measure based on the relative ranks of firms at two different points. We consider the beginning and the end of the period for such an analysis. This measure is defined as the standard deviation of $q_i = r_i/r_{i*}$, where r_i is the rank of firm i at the end of a period and r_{i*} is its rank at the beginning of the period. The standard deviation of 'q' is an indicator of the average amount of shifting in rank during the period. It may be noted that higher the value of the standard deviation of q (Ijiri–Simon Index), higher the competition and vice versa. It is also to be noted that q becomes 0 if all the relative ranks are the same and q_i takes the value 1 for all the industry groups.

Another polar case for Ijri–Simon Index is discussed below.

$$r_i^* = n - r_i$$

$$q_i = \frac{n - r_i^*}{r_i^*} = \frac{n}{r_i^*} - 1$$

$$SD\ (q_i) = n.SD\ (\frac{1}{r_i^*})$$

$$= SD\ (\frac{1}{r_i^*})$$

We have carried out this exercise, as suggested by Ijiri and Simon, for all the 14 industries for the two consecutive years at the beginning, 1988–9 and 1989–90, as well as at the end, 1999–2000 and 2000–1, of the period of analysis. The results are given in Table 2.3.

From Table 2.3 it can be seen that in six out of 14 industries, the average shifting has come down, suggesting that competition has declined. Out of the remaining eight industries, for one industry (Electrical Machinery), the average shifting remained the same while for the other seven industries it has increased. This suggests that only in these seven industries competition has increased. The decline in competition varies from 18 per cent to 60 per cent while the increase ranges from 13 to 304 per cent. Again, while average

[17] Ijiri and Simon (1977).

shifting in the initial period ranges from 0.002 to 0.051; in the end period it ranges from 0.002 to 0.042 implying a decline in the average rate of shifting (upper value). It is also to be noted that the highest average shifting in the initial year was in the Metal Products industry (0.051), the lowest was in Cotton Textiles followed by Non-electrical Machinery. In the end period, it was again Metal Products (0.042), but the lowest being Beverage & Tobacco industry followed by Non-electrical Machinery. It is to be noted that the ISI values in columns 2 and 3 in Table 2.3 are quite close to the polar value of 0. This is due to the use of the new turnover index, which is truncated within the interval 0 to 1.

Table 2.3
Ijiri-Simon Index (ISI) of Competition by Industry
(1988–9/1989–90 and 1999–2000/2000–1)

Industry	Standard Deviation of Relative Ranks		
	1989–90/1988–9	2000–1/1999–2000	% Change
1	2	3	4
Beverage & Tobacco	0.005 (4.5)	0.002 (1)	–60.0
Cotton Textiles	0.002 (2)	0.003 (3.5)	50.0
Drugs & Pharmaceuticals	0.036 (12)	0.021 (10)	–41.7
Electrical Machinery	0.040 (13)	0.040 (13)	0.0
Electronics	0.011 (7)	0.037 (12)	236.4
Food Products	0.015 (8)	0.017 (7)	13.3
Iron & Steel	0.005 (4.5)	0.003 (3.5)	–40.0
Metal Products	0.051 (14)	0.042 (14)	–17.6
Non-electrical Machinery	0.0018 (1)	0.0022 (2)	22.2
Non-ferrous Metals	0.0102 (6)	0.0234 (11)	129.4
Non-metallic Minerals	0.0167(9)	0.0202 (9)	21.0
Synthetic Textiles	0.0311 (11)	0.0167 (6)	–46.3
Transport Equipment	0.022 (10)	0.009 (5)	–59.1
Wood & Paper	0.0046 (3)	0.0186 (8)	304.3
Average for All Industries	0.0180	0.0182	
Correlation between col. 2 and col. 3 = 0.699			

Sources: CMIE, Prowess, (2005), GoI [CSO] (1992).
Note: Figures in parentheses are the ranks.

The following trend in average shifting is worth noting. The largest decline in the average shifting (–60.0 per cent) was in Beverages & Tobacco. The smallest decline occurred in the Metal Products industry (–17.6 per cent). The largest increase in average shifting occurred in the Wood & Paper industry while the smallest increase was observed in the Food Products industry. This suggests that the pace of increase/decrease in competition also varies widely among the industries.

To understand whether competitive industries remained competitive or became non-competitive and vice versa, we have calculated rank correlation coefficients between the average shifting at the two end points in Table 2.3. We get a rank correlation of 0.70, suggesting that the position of industries in relation to competition or non-competition does not seem to have changed very much. Since average shifting for all industries has also remained almost the same (0.0180 and 0.0182), it shows that no substantial change in the structure of competition has occurred during the period.

Mobility and Size Structure

The rank correlation analysis based on the new turnover index and the average shifting measured by the Ijiri–Simon Index have provided some indication of the presence of competition in the industries. But this does not provide any indication of the impact of mobility on size structure. In order to get insights into this, we estimate standard measures based on the moments of the frequency distributions of industries such as the coefficient of variation, skewness, and kurtosis for the end points for all the industries as reported in Table 2.4.

Skewness is a measure of the lack of symmetry in a distribution, that is, whether the distribution is skewed to the left or the right.

A measure of skewness is given by,

$$\mu_3 = E\,(x - \mu)^3$$

where μ is the mean and μ_3 is the 3rd central moment.

If the distribution is symmetric, μ_3 will be equal to zero. If the distribution is skewed to the left, μ_3 will be negative, and if the distribution is skewed right, then μ_3 will be positive.

$\mu_3 < 0$ Negatively skewed | $\mu_3 = 0$ Symmetrical | $\mu_3 > 0$ Positively skewed

Table 2.4
Changes in the Coefficient of Variation, Skewness, and Kurtosis of Size by Industry (1988–9 and 2000–1)

Industry	CV		Skewness		Kurtosis	
	1988–9	2000–1	1988–9	2000–1	1988–9	2000–1
Beverage & Tobacco	1.77	2.87	3.43	3.71	12.34	13.81
Cotton Textiles	3.62	3.19	6.93	6.71	48.90	46.73
Drugs & Pharmaceuticals	1.02	1.55	2.47	3.50	5.91	13.96
Electrical Machinery	1.26	1.34	3.07	2.24	11.85	5.09
Electronics	2.41	1.65	3.57	2.07	13.24	3.94
Food Products	1.21	1.18	2.60	2.10	7.55	5.20
Iron & Steel	3.60	2.48	4.73	3.60	22.94	13.94
Metal Products	1.11	1.33	1.27	2.18	0.19	5.60
Non-electrical Machinery	3.62	3.06	6.83	6.63	49.35	47.43
Non-ferrous Metals	2.16	1.32	3.39	1.25	12.38	0.20
Non-metallic Minerals	1.73	1.85	3.22	3.27	10.45	10.16
Synthetic Textiles	1.15	1.14	1.82	1.95	3.03	3.61
Transport Equipment	2.05	2.17	3.52	3.44	13.44	13.27
Wood & Paper	2.21	1.13	3.98	1.48	16.70	1.04

Sources: CMIE, Prowess, (2005), GoI [CSO] (1992).
Note: CV: Coefficient of variation.

Kurtosis is the degree of 'peakedness' of a distribution, defined as a normalized form of the fourth central moment of a distribution. The formula is given by,

$$\beta_2 = \frac{\mu_4}{\mu_2^2}$$

where μ_4 is the 4th central moment and μ_2 is the variance.

A distribution with a high peak is called *leptokurtic*, a flat-topped curve is called *platykurtic*, and the normal distribution is called *mesokurtic*.

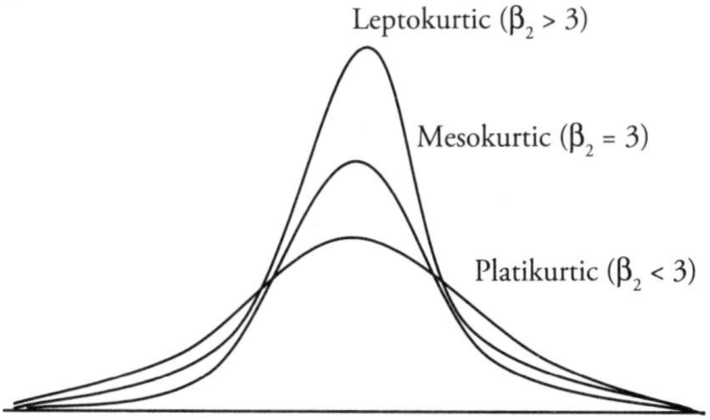

The coefficient of variation of size has increased in six industries, substantially in Beverages & Tobacco and Drug & Pharmaceuticals, and decreased in the remaining eight industries, notably in Non-ferrous Metals and Wood & Paper. Next, we examine how strong have these trends been in concentration, as indicated by the skewness of the distribution.

The interesting feature of the distribution levels is that all of them are skewed to the right both in the initial and terminal year as indicated by the positive value of the third moment. In other words, in all the industries there is a concentration of firms in the smaller size classes for both periods. The asymmetry has increased only in five industries: Beverages & Tobacco, Drug & Pharmaceuticals, Metal Products, Non-Metallic Minerals, and Synthetic Textiles. In the case of peaked levels, as measured by Kurtosis, it has increased in four industries and decreased in the remaining ten. In other words, in majority of the cases, the peaked levels have decreased.

The analysis of the moments of the distribution levels clearly shows that mobility analysis is incomplete unless we examine the nature of size structure in general and inter- and intra- size class (Net Assets) mobility of firms in particular.

This is accomplished by undertaking analysis of transition matrices of all the industries, which alone can capture the nuances of firm mobility. This is illustrated with the transition pattern of firms in one of the industries, Synthetic Textiles[18] (See Table 2.5).

Now we proceed to draw the transition matrix of firms, where frequency distribution of firms by decile-wise size-class is estimated for the end points, that is, 1988–9 and 2000–1. Each size-class is taken as double the previous size class in order to capture not only substantial mobility but also enable sharper and clearer interpretation of size and growth. It may be noted that we have taken 5 per cent as a separate size class (though strictly it does not fall within the decile definition) considering the size distribution of firms in our sample. While this analysis basically follows Hart and Prais,[19] Singh and Whittington,[20] etc., we have improved upon

[18] Similar transition matrices have been calculated for all the 13 industries, but the results are not reported due to space limitation.

[19] Hart and Prais (1956).

[20] Singh and Whittington (1968).

their methodology by taking deciles instead of size-class *per se* in order to ensure comparability across time.

Table 2.5
Transition Matrix of Firms in Synthetic Textiles by Size-class, 1988–9 to 2000–1

Size-Class (Decile-wise) (1988–9) / Size-class (Decile-wise) (2000–1)	≤ 5	>5-10	>10-20	>20-40	>40-80	>80	Total No. of firms in 1988–9
≤ 5	4	1	–	1	–	–	6
>5<-≤10	2	–	3	2	–	–	7
>10-≤20	–	2	–	–	–	–	2
>20-≤40	–	–	–	1	1	1	3
>40-≤80	–	–	1	1	1	–	3
>80	–	–	–	–	–	1	1
Total No. of firms in 2000–1	6	3	4	5	2	2	22

Sources: CMIE, Prowess, (2005), GoI [CSO] (1992).

Firstly, the transition matrix (TM) shows whether the size distribution of firms has changed or not during the period as indicated by the frequency of the size-class given in the last row and the last column. For example, only in the case of the first size class, the frequency remains the same. Secondly, TM provides the number of firms, which moved upward/downward and/or remained in the same size-class. The diagonal element shows the number of firms without inter-class mobility during the period. The left of the diagonal in any row indicates downward inter-class mobility and the right upward inter-class mobility. It may be noted that in the first row only upward mobility is possible since it begins with the diagonal element. Similarly, in the case of the last but one row only downward mobility is possible since it ends with the diagonal element. As a result, both upward and downward mobility can be captured only in the rows between the first and the last. For example, all the firms in the size-class (first decile-class, second row) in 1988–9 have moved out either to the higher or lower size-class by 2000–1. More precisely, three moved to 2nd decile-class, two to fourth decile-class, and the remaining two moved down to ≤.5 class by the end of the period.

Another noteworthy feature of the mobility analysis is that it clearly shows that the identity of firms in a size-class can change even when frequency remains the same. This is best brought out from the first size-class itself. The number of firms is six in the first size-class at the beginning as well as at the terminal year. But the transition matrix shows that two out of the six firms in the year 1988–9 moved out, one to the second decile and another to the fourth decile. Another two firms from the second decile moved into the first size-class leaving the size-class frequency constant. Thus, the six firms in 2000–1 are not the same six in 1988–9. This changing identity can happen in any size-class even when there is no change in the frequency within the size-class. The nature of this problem for the remaining industries will be examined later.

Mobility and Market Structure

In addition to the identity of firms in the size-class, the mobility analysis has implication for the market structure. It depends on the nature and direction of mobility. If mobility is only in one direction, say upward, then industry is getting more and more concentrated. If it is in either direction, upward and downward, the firms move towards an efficient scale according to traditional theory of the firm under profit maximization.

If the mobility is intra-class but not inter-class and restricted to smaller classes, then it indicates the features of dominant-firm-with-fringe competition (DFFC). The DFFC model can be illustrated using the transition matrix of the Food Products industry given in Table 2.6.

The mobility of firms is concentrated in the left-hand top corner of the matrix and within the first two deciles (10 and 20) of the size distribution. Size-rank test of the industry shows that competition among firms in the smaller classes is high but low in the upper deciles. This is also statistically valid.[21] This is an indication that

[21] See Pushpangadan and Shanta (2004).

market structure is of the DFFC competition. Of course, the market structure is confirmed only if the price-taking behaviour of the firms, as suggested by Basu (1993), is found valid. This is beyond the scope of the present analysis. Let us extend the analysis to all the industries so that main features of dynamic competition can be captured.

Table 2.6
Transition Matrix of Firms in Food Products by Size-class, 1988–9 to 2000–1

Size-Class (Decile-wise) (1988–9) / Size-class (Decile-wise) (2000–1)	≤ 5	>5-10	>10-20	>20-40	>40-80	>80	Total No. of firms in 1988–9
≤ 5	8	3	2	–	1	–	14
>5<-≤10	3	3	–	1	2	–	9
>10-≤20	3	2	4	–	-	–	9
>20-≤40	–	1	1	1	1	–	4
>40-≤80	–	–	1	1	2	–	4
>80	–	–	–	–	–	1	1
Total No. of firms in 2000–1	14	9	8	3	6	1	41

Sources: CMIE, Prowess, (2005), GoI [CSO] (1992).

The first feature is the changing nature of the size-structure of industries. It may be noted that the class-interval has been reduced to three instead of six in the earlier transition matrices due to inadequate number of firms within each size-class. However, here again each decile class is taken as double the previous decile class in order to have geometric intervals, as done in the transition matrices. As stated earlier, this helps to capture not only substantial mobility but also enables sharper and clearer interpretation of size and growth. The change in the size distribution of firms arising out of the transition process[22] for the end points is shown in Table 2.7.

[22] These transition matrices will be made available on request.

Table 2.7
Frequency Distributions by Size-class and by Industry, 1988–9 and 2000–1

Industry	Year	≤ 2nd decile 0–20	>2nd decile and ≤ 4th decile 20–40	>4th decile 40+
Beverage & Tobacco	1988–9	92.9(13)	–	7.1(1)
	2000–1	92.9(13)	–	7.1(1)
Cotton Textiles	1988–9	98(50)	–	2(1)
	2000–1	98.1(50)	–	1.9(1)
Drugs & Pharmaceuticals	1988–9	56.7(17)	33.3(10)	10(3)
	2000–1	86.7(26)	3.3 (1)	10(3)
Electrical Machinery	1988–9	80.8(38)	12.8(6)	6.4(3)
	2000–1	74.5(35)	10.6(5)	14.9(7)
Electronics	1988–9	90(27)	3.3(1)	6.7(2)
	2000–1	80(24)	3.3(1)	16.7(5)
Food Products	1988–9	78(32)	9.8(4)	12.2(5)
	2000–1	75.7(31)	7.3(3)	17(7)
Iron & Steel	1988–9	96(24)	–	4(1)
	2000–1	88(22)	4(1)	8(2)
Metal Products	1988–9	63.6(14)	13.6(3)	22.7(5)
	2000–1	68.2(15)	13.6(3)	18.1(4)
Non-electric Machinery	1988–9	96.6(57)	1.7(1)	1.7(1)
	2000–1	96.6(57)	1.7(1)	1.7(1)
Non-ferrous Metal	1988–9	81.3(13)	12.5(2)	6.2(1)
	2000–1	62.5(10)	12.5(2)	25(4)
Non-metallic Minerals	1988–9	91.6(44)	2.1(1)	6.3(3)
	2000–1	89.5(43)	4.2(2)	6.3(3)
Synthetic Textiles	1988–9	68.3 (15)	13.6 (3)	18.1(4)
	2000–1	59.1(13)	22.7(5)	18.2(4)
Transport Equipment	1988–9	88.8(64)	5.6(4)	5.6(4)
	2000–1	89(64)	4.2(3)	7(5)
Wood & Paper	1988–9	90(18)	5(1)	5(1)
	2000–1	55(11)	25(5)	20(4)

Sources: CMIE, Prowess, (2005), GoI [CSO] (1992).
Note: Figures in the parentheses are the number of firms in each size-class.

The frequencies of all size-classes have changed in four industries (Electrical Machinery, Food Products, Iron & Steel, and Wood & Paper). It is to be observed that in six industries out of 14, that is, for about 43 per cent, there is no change in the number of firms in the large size-class. This does not, however, rule out the mobility of firms from the largest decile to other deciles and vice versa. That is, there can be identity changes as observed earlier in the case of Synthetic Textiles. Of the six industries with the same number of firms in the largest size-class (>80) during the period, in three industries (Synthetic Textiles, Drug & Pharmaceuticals, and Non-metallic Minerals) there is change in the identity of firms. In these industries, the conventional concentration ratios (n-firm market shares) could remain the same but mobility has occurred. This clearly establishes the superiority of the new turnover index over the market share or n-firm concentration ratio. It provides important insights on inter- and intra-class mobility which alone can give an accurate picture of the nature of competition in an industry.[23]

Baldwin (1998) discusses the superiority of the turnover index over concentration ratios in detail. He considers concentration ratios and market structure statistics as static measures. To him they capture only what happens outside the box while inside the box the competitive process is at work, as firms constantly vie for competitive advantage. In other words, there is more than one dimension to the competitive process. He sums up the results of his analysis as follows: 'Concentration and mobility measures have been treated as substitutes, rather than complements. This reflects, in part, the preoccupation of economists with finding a relatively simple concentration measure to use as a straight-forward index that can guage the state of competition and the lack of effort devoted to measuring the internal dynamics of markets. The intensity of competition in the real world is not amenable to simplification because there is such a wide variety of events occurring within individual industries. The concentration and mobility indices are related, but imperfectly. They reveal different aspects of the competitive process. In order to detect those industries where competition problems may arise, mobility and concentration indices need to be used together.'[24]

The second issue, most important from the standpoint of industrial organization theory, is the insight given by mobility analysis on the market structure and size-distribution. Although there is no integration of the two in the traditional literature, which is still an

[23] For a detailed work on mobility analysis, see Baldwin (1998).

[24] Concentration ratios were found related to entry and exit of firms but not with changes in the incumbent population (Baldwin 1998).

unresolved issue as far as industrial economists are concerned, one model that is, which integrates the two DFFC. In such models, the size-structure will be skewed to the right and with high intra-mobility within the smaller size-classes but very little inter-mobility between the small and the large classes. One industry that has such market structure is the Food Products as demonstrated earlier.[25] It may be noted that under *u*-shaped average cost curves, competitive market structure should have both upward and downward mobility. Since all such interesting patterns of mobility cannot be put down for each industry, we provide a summary of the mobility patterns of all the industries during the period in Table 2.8.

Table 2.8
Nature of Mobility of Firms by Industries, 1988–9/2000–1

Industry	Mobility across Size-classes* (Proportion of firms in each category)		
	No Mobility	Upward	Downward
1	2	3	4
Beverage & Tobacco	0.64	0.00	0.36
Cotton Textiles	0.82	0.13	0.04
Drugs & Pharmaceuticals	0.13	0.07	0.80
Electric Machinery	0.45	0.32	0.23
Electronics	0.70	0.23	0.07
Food Products	0.46	0.24	0.29
Iron & Steel	0.72	0.24	0.04
Metal Products	0.36	0.23	0.41
Non-electrical Machinery	0.86	0.12	0.02
Non-ferrous Metal	0.50	0.44	0.06
Non-metallic Minerals	0.46	0.33	0.21
Synthetic Textiles	0.32	0.41	0.27
Transport Equipment	0.82	0.05	0.13
Wood & Paper	0.35	0.60	0.05
Average for All Industries	0.55	0.24	0.21

Sources: CMIE, Prowess, (2005), GoI [CSO] (1992).
Note: *(column 2+ column 3+ column 4) = 1.

Table 2.8 provides estimates on the percentage of firms moving in the upward direction, downward direction, and remaining in the same size-class by industries during the period. It may be noted that on an average 54 per cent of the firms remain in the same class,

[25] See Pushpangadan and Shanta (2004) for an empirical test.

24 per cent move upward, and 21 per cent downward in the manufacturing sector. Further, the highest percentage of firms remaining in the same class is in the Non-electrical Machinery (86 per cent) with Cotton Textiles and Transport Equipment showing the same high levels of immobility (82 per cent). The highest upward mobility has occurred in Wood & Paper whereas in the case of downward mobility, it is in Drugs & Pharmaceuticals. Beverage & Tobacco does not show any upward mobility and Non-electrical Machinery indicates very little downward mobility.

If the competitive pressure were high in an industry, then it would have higher mobility in either direction under *u*-shaped cost-curves in the long run. This implies that the measures of competition and mobility should be positively related among the industries.

Three versions of the same hypothesis can be formulated if the average cost curves is not of the conventional type. They are: (i) upward mobility alone is positively related to competition; (ii) downward mobility is alone positively related to competition; and (iii) both upward and downward mobility are positively related to competition.

Empirical evidence is reported in Figures 2.1(a), 2.1(b), and 2.1(c) with correlation coefficients. Note that the competition is measured by the Ijiri–Simon index for the endpoint (1999–2001) and the mobility of firms for the entire period. The results show that only the correlation coefficient between total mobility index (upward+downward) given in Figure 2.1(c) and competitive index is statistically significant. In other words, more competition prevails in industries with mobility in either direction; otherwise it is not. This proves that as mentioned in the literature, it is the mixing and reordering of firms that constitutes vigorous/effective competition.

The analysis implies that public policy for increasing competition should address ways and means of removing mobility barriers in the manufacturing sector.

SUMMARY AND CONCLUSIONS

Competition, being multidimensional in nature, needs to be looked at from different angles. As mentioned earlier, the mobility of firms is identified as one with the capacity for dynamic and effective competition. At the same time it is also not without criticism. The

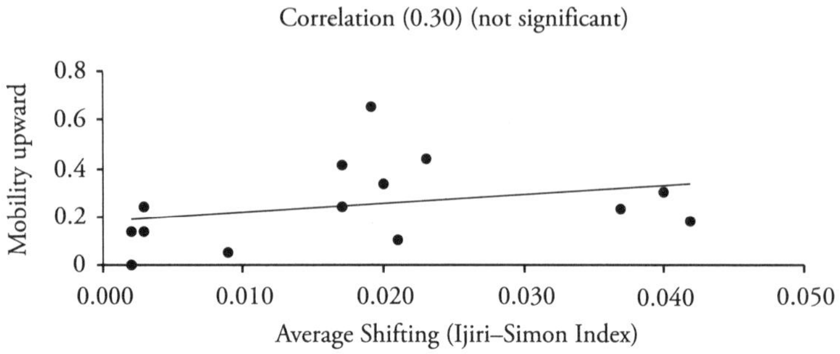

Figure 2.1 (a): Upward Mobility and Average Shifting

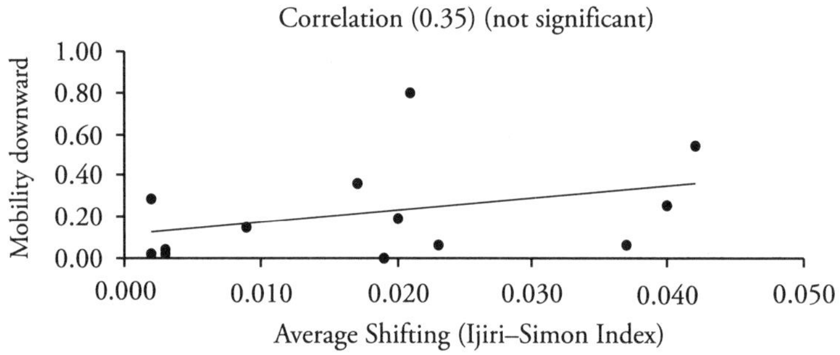

Figure 2.1 (b): Downward Mobility and Average Shifting

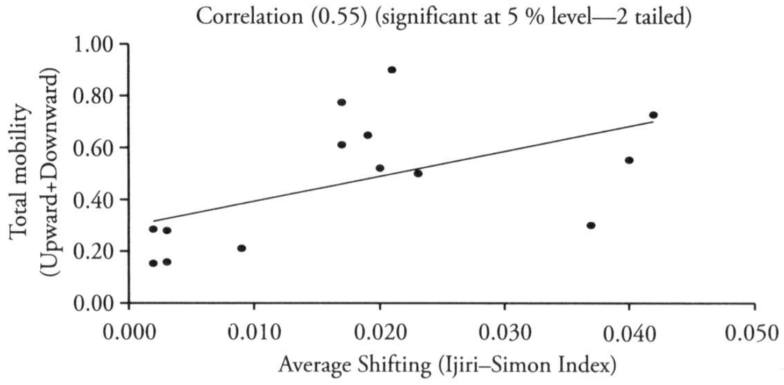

Figure 2.1 (c): Mobility and Average Shifting

Figure 2.1: Mobility and Ijiri-Simon Index of Competition, All Industries (2000-01/1999-2000)

main criticism against the turnover index (the rank ordering of size) is that it only shows whether the size of a firm is larger or smaller than that of another firm but not by how much. Therefore, the instability of the ranks may not capture the extent of competition. The second criticism is that the changes in market shares which are the really significant phenomenon for understanding the market does not get reflected in the rank analysis.

The contention of this chapter is that if the limitations of the turnover index are taken care of, it can provide several important insights on competition, which cannot be captured by other indicators, such as the concentration ratio and is therefore an important tool for public policy.

In this chapter, we provide an alternative turnover index, which overcomes the limitations of the traditional index through an order preserving transformation of the data provided by CMIE (Prowess) on 14 major industries for the period 1998–9/2000–1. This chapter clearly establishes that mixing and reordering, upward, and downward mobility of firms in an industry is an important dimension of what constitutes effective competition—a dynamic dimension. Testing the new index for rank shifts in the Indian context for 14 industries, we get the following results on the state of competition in manufacturing industries: The stability between the ranks of the industries for the end points indicates that 43 per cent of the industry groups accounting for 70 per cent of net value added of all sample firms have very low mobility, thus implying low competition. It is also observed that mobility improves over a longer period. The change in competition examined through Ijiri–Simon index indicating average shifting among firms belonging to 14 industrial groups shows that 50 per cent of the Industry groups accounting for 49 per cent of net value added of all sample firms have shown an increasing trend. But the rank correlation of change in competition or average shifting among the industries over the period does not show any shift in their relative positions during the period. This implies that some rigidity exists in the expansion of competitive forces in the manufacturing sector.

The changing nature of the size-structure is examined by the skewness and kurtosis of the distributions. The frequencies of all size-classes have changed in four industries (Food Products, Iron

& Steel, Electrical Machinery, and Wood & Paper). It is observed that in six industries out of 14, about 50 per cent, there is no change in the number of firms in the large size-classes. This does not, however, rule out the mobility of firms from the largest to other smaller classes and vice versa. In other words, the identity of firms in a class can change even when the frequency does not change. Of the six industries with same number of firms in the largest size-class (>80) during the period, three of them (Drugs & Pharmaceuticals, Non-metallic Minerals and Synthetic Textiles) exhibit change in the identities. In these industries it may be noted the concentration ratios could remain the same and yet mobility could occur indicating competition.

The inter- and intra-class mobility of firms is examined for its implication for market structure using transition matrices. The analysis gives the following conclusions. On an average, 55 per cent of the firms remain in the same class, again suggesting low competition; 24 per cent move upward and 21 per cent downward in the manufacturing sector. Further, the highest percentage of firms remaining in the same class is in the Non-electrical Machinery (86 per cent) with Cotton Textiles and Transport Equipment showing the same high levels of immobility (82 per cent). The highest upward mobility has occurred in Wood & Paper whereas in the case of downward mobility it is in Drugs & Pharmaceuticals. Beverages & Tobacco does not show any upward mobility and Non-electrical Machinery indicates very little downward mobility. The study also links up patterns of mobility with market structure. It illustrates the existence of varied types of competition in terms of inter- and intra-class mobility, which cannot be captured by the traditional concentration ratios. It shows that competition is not associated with either upward or downward mobility but only with both.

This chapter has also shown that with the new turnover index, size-rank changes and share changes are related. However, the processes underlying the market share changes are not captured. This question is taken up in detail in Chapter 3 including the integration of mobility and concentration measures as emphasized by Baldwin (1998).

APPENDIX 2A

The Order Preserving Turnover Index and Market Share Instability

The objective here is to show that one major criticism leveled against the turnover index, namely, that it shows nothing about market share instability is not tenable if the firms are ranked after adjusting for the actual differences of the sizes through an order preserving transformation. The empirical validity of this proposition is tested for the set of fourteen manufacturing industry groups in India for 1989–2001.

Equation (2.2) in Chapter 2 clearly showed that the transformed variable of firm j is linearly related to its market share of assets.

The relationship of these coefficients with the changes in market shares is verified using the Hymer and Pashigian (HP) instability index[1] and discussed in the text. We use total net assets to measure size as well as for calculating market shares.

The Empirical Results

The correlation coefficients between the order preserving transformation of size relating to the two years, 1988–9 and 2000–1, have been estimated for fourteen industry groups in India. The HP index is also calculated for the same industries for the period 1988–9/2000–1. Then we test whether market shares instability and turnover index are correlated. The results are given in Table 2A.1.

It is interesting to note that rank correlation coefficients from the traditional turnover index and new turnover index by industry groups are widely different except in the case of synthetic textiles and transport equipment. The correlation coefficient between the two turnover indices and the market share instability index are negatively related. It is statistically significant only in the case of new turnover index. (It is to be noted that while HP concludes from their data that there is little relationship between the turnover index and the instability index, they do not provide evidence of any statistical testing).[2]

The most important finding is that the correlation coefficients between the new turnover index based on the order preserving transformation and the market share instability index are negatively related and significant

[1] Hymer and Pashigian (1962), p. 85.

[2] We have statistically tested the relationship for HP data given in their table 4 and found that the Pearson correlation coefficient is –0.19 (excluding mergers) and –0.13 (including mergers) and is negative and insignificant.

Table 2A.1
Correlation Coefficients and Market Share Instability Index by Industry (1988–9 and 2000–1)

Industry	Rank Correlation Coefficient (Traditional Turn-over Index)	Rank Correlation Coefficient (New Turnover Index)	Market Share Instability Index
1	2	3	4
Beverage & Tobacco	0.77	0.98	0.88
Cotton Textiles	0.43	0.98	1.38
Drugs & Pharmaceuticals	0.65	0.59	1.55
Electrical Machinery	0.82	0.88	1.48
Electronics	0.86	0.57	1.47
Food Products	0.51	0.68	1.36
Iron & Steel	0.76	0.93	0.85
Metal Products	0.71	0.55	1.57
Non-electrical Machinery	0.83	0.99	0.85
Non-ferrous Metals	0.81	0.57	1.35
Non-metallic Minerals	0.63	0.42	1.40
Synthetic Textiles	0.70	0.72	1.59
Transport Equipment	0.84	0.85	1.43
Wood & Paper	0.82	0.65	1.36
Pearson Correlation Coefficient	(Col. 2 and Col. 4) –0.21	(Col. 3 and Col. 4) –0.63*	

Source: CMIE (2001).
Note: * Significant at 5 per cent level.

at 5 per cent level (–0.63). Thus, our analysis clearly shows that Hymer–Pashigian's conclusion—that the turnover measure shows nothing about changes in market shares—does not hold good. On the other hand, our analysis indicates a close relationship between the transformed variables and market shares. In other words, the new transformed index overcomes the criticisms against the traditional turnover index, that it, is not reflective of market changes.

3

Concentration

An Integrated Approach to Static and Dynamic Aspects

Analysing to get insights on the patterns of market share changes, an important structural dimension of the competitive struggle, is the crux of this chapter. This is because, quite in contrast to the traditional theory which associated competition with large number of sellers and buyers, in a fast changing world of innovation, imitation, etc., it is possible to come across wide-ranging market structures (ranging from contestable and oligopolistic markets to large number of firms colluding with each other to set the price) which have implications for competition policy—so much so that share cutting can take various patterns. Static and dynamic measures of concentration reveal different aspects of the competitive process. Therefore, either of these measures used in isolation cannot capture the variety of competitive processes at work. The two measures need to be used in conjunction with each other rather than separately because the information they produce is complementary.

This can be achieved only by integrating the two measures. For this, the state and process of competition needs to be related. Theoretically we have seen that innovation, the driving force behind competition, is what bridges the static and dynamic aspects of the competitive process (Baumol 2002). This chapter is therefore an attempt to integrate static and dynamic measures of competition/concentration for understanding the underlying processes.

The chapter is divided into four sections. Section 1 reviews the literature. Section 2 deals with a model that integrates static and dynamic measure of concentration. Section 3 gives the empirical results, followed by a summary and conclusions in the last section.

REVIEW OF LITERATURE

The purpose of this review is to find the appropriate method by which it is possible to assess the vigour of competition or the nature of share cutting in an industry. While there are several studies based on either static measures (concentration ratios) or dynamic measures to understand competition, there are very few studies which have attempted to measure share cutting. There are only two studies, that of Gort (1963) and Grossack (1965), which have attempted to measure share cutting.

The main objectives of Gort's study are: (i) to present new information on stability and change in market shares of leading firms, (ii) to examine the reasons for stability in shares particularly with other aspects of market structure, and (iii) to explore the consequences of stability for industry profit rates. Among these issues, the most relevant to our study is the method used by Gort to examine if the growth in the market share of large firms is at the expense of small firms or vice versa, using data from the Census of Manufactures for the years 1947 and 1954, relating to 205 manufacturing industries in the US. Analysis was restricted to the firms that were among the leading 15 in either or both of the years mentioned above. Thus, the sample included firms that generally grew faster than average (those that entered the class of leading 15 in 1954) as well as those that on the whole grow less than average (firms that left the class of leading 15). The maximum number of observations for any industry was 26 and the modal number 19. The data employed restricts the analysis to firms, which might be considered either large or medium-sized for their industries, and this is considered the size range in which stability of shares is most relevant for analysis of competitive structure. Two measures of stability are used: (i) the rank correlation coefficient of the shares in 1947 and 1954; and (ii) the geometric mean of the regression coefficients of shares in 1954 on 1947 and its reciprocal regression coefficient in 1947 on 1954.

The first measure tells us the extent to which the shares at one point in time are dependent on those at another point. The second measure was designed to overcome the bias that affects either of the two regression coefficients taken separately—a bias that arises from the general tendency of firms that are largest at the end of a period to have grown more than the average, and of those that are largest at the outset to grow less than average in the future. Accordingly coefficients of more than unity were taken to signify on the average a growth in the market shares of large firms at the expense of the smaller ones, while coefficients that are less than unity signified the opposite. This is the closest approximation to the understanding of the issue under hand, namely share cutting that this method gives. We do not go into the details of the empirical results. The utility of this method for our analysis is limited since it says nothing of whether large firms lost to each other (and by how much) etc. The answer to our query was found in Grossack's model.

According to Grossack (1965), the use of changes in market shares of individual firms in the analysis of monopoly power when analytically incorporated with static measures, prove to be of great help in identifying and understanding monopoly power. In this context Grossack develops a model, which satisfies the two requirements of measuring concentration and capturing share cutting. Such a model or measure of structural change particularly suits our enquiry for understanding the processes and the vigour of competition. We apply this model to Indian data.

THE MODEL

The essence of Grossack's (1965) model is as follows: to infer the existence of monopoly power a dynamic measure of structural change is necessary. In other words, such a measure should reveal: (i) whether large firms of some 'initial' years have been able to maintain their market shares up to some 'terminal' year; (ii) whether large firms have lost their share to small firms, new entrants, or to other large firms. To capture these requirements, he used the regression coefficient obtained by estimating the regression of market shares in the terminal year of all firms on the initial year.

This is defined as follows:

$$b = \frac{\sum x_i y_i}{\sum x_i^2}$$

where $x_i y_i$ are the deviations of the market share of the firm i from the mean for the initial year 'X' and terminal year 'Y' respectively. Alternatively, the above regression coefficient can be rewritten as:

$$b = 1 + \sum_i w_i \left(\frac{y_i - x_i}{x_i} \right)$$

where

$$w_i = \frac{x_i^2}{\sum x_i^2}$$

The following comments/observations on the formula are in order. As evident from the definition, the distinct characteristics of this measure are that it gives more weight to the larger firms of the initial year in determining the value[1] of b. Following this, it can be interpreted that if $b>1$, concentration has increased, if $b<1$ it has decreased, and if equal to one no change has occurred. The logic underlying this is that an increase in the share of an above average size firm and a decrease in the share of a below average size firm will give a value of $b>1$. Similarly the movement of a firm's share towards the mean market share will give a value of $b<1$.

But the value of b alone will not help to understand the movement of the shares across size classes. To capture this, Grossack has devised an ingenious decomposition exercise wherein the regression coefficient (which we call the static and dynamic or SD index) is expressed as a product of the rank correlation coefficient of market shares and the change in concentration ratio. By doing this, he also achieves an integration of the static and dynamic measures of concentration and overcomes the limitations of using either one of these measures in isolation.[2] The derivation of this formula is given below.

$$b = \frac{\Sigma x_i y_i}{\Sigma x_i^2} = r * \frac{\sigma_y}{\sigma_x} \tag{3.1}$$

[1] This is justified on the basis of the fact that it is the large firms that have the power to enhance (short-run) prices.

[2] This is the analytical achievement of Grossack over Gort's method.

where r is the coefficient of correlation of the market shares in the two years, and σ_x and σ_y are the standard deviations of the shares in the respective years. Two points of equation (3.1) are relevant for our analysis. The first one is how the standard deviation, σ_x/σ_y, relates to the concentration ratio of the industry. It can be shown that it is related to the most commonly used standard measure of concentration, Herfindahl Index, in the literature, which is defined as,

$$HI(X) = \sum_i x_i^2 + 1/n \qquad (3.1a)$$

$$HI(Y) = \sum_i y_i^2 + 1/n \qquad (3.1b)$$

where n is the sample size in an industry.

It can be observed from equations 3.1a and 3.1b, that concentration increases with either greater variation in the sizes of the firms or with a smaller number of firms.[3] This is true both in the initial and terminal years. The second point is to show that the ratio of standard deviation of the terminal year to that in the initial year reflects change in concentration ratio. By definition,

$$\frac{\sigma_y}{\sigma_x} = \sqrt{\sum y_i^2 \Big/ \sum x_i^2} \qquad (3.1c)$$

Substituting (3.1a), (3.1b) in (3.1c), we have,

$$\frac{\sigma_y}{\sigma_x} = \sqrt{\frac{HI(Y) - 1/n}{HI(X) - 1/n}}$$

when n becomes large,

$$\frac{\sigma_y}{\sigma_x} \approx \sqrt{HI(Y) \big/ HI(X)} = \sqrt{C(HI)} \qquad (3.2)$$

where $C(HI)$ = HI(Y)/HI(X)

Substituting (3.2) in (3.1) we have,

$$b \approx r\sqrt{C(HI)} \qquad (3.3)$$

[3] Grossack (1965), p. 302.

The derivation in equation (3.3) shows that the regression coefficient of y_i on x_i can be approximated by the product of the correlation of shares and change in the concentration ratio measured by Herfindahl Index (square root). It also emphasizes that share cutting has to be interpreted both in relation to concentration ratios and correlation between the market shares in the two years.

From equation (3.3), four categories of industries can be distinguished depending on the value of *b* and its two components,[4] *r* and √C(HI), as indicated below:

1. If $b>1$ and the value of *r* close to unity, then it implies increase in concentration;
2. If $b<1$ three situations can be distinguished depending on the value of *r* and √C(HI): (i) *r* is low and √C(HI) approximately equal to 1 implying large firms lost market to each other; (ii) *r* is high and √C(HI) is low implying large firms as a group lost market shares to small firms; and (iii) both low, implying large firms lost market shares to each other and to small firms.

THE EMPIRICAL RESULTS

The Data

As stated at the outset, the database for the empirical analysis and the choice of the industries is the same as that of Chapter 2.

The Results

To understand the existence of monopoly power and other dimensions associated with the model, we have calculated HI, *b* and *r* of the model for a short period, with initial year 1988–9 and terminal year 1994–5, and for a long period taking 1988–9 as the initial year and 2000–1 as the terminal year. The results are given in Table 3.1.

Table 3.1 gives the Herfindahl Index (*HI*) for the years 1988–9, 1994–5, and 2000–1; the regression coefficient *b*, for the short and long period; the correlation coefficient of market shares *r* and the square root of the change in the Herfindahl Index, √C(HI), for the short and long periods. This table shows that for all industry

[4] Ibid., p. 305.

Table 3.1
Industry-wise Static and Dynamic Measures of Structural Change
(1988–9 to 1994–5 and 1988–9 to 2000–1)

Industry	*HI*			*b*		*r*		√C(HI)		√C(HI)*r	
	1989	1995	2001	89–95	89–01	89–95	89–01	89–95	89–01	89–95	89–01
Beverage & Tobacco	0.27	0.43	0.53	1.24	1.38	0.94	0.92	1.24	1.40	1.17	1.27
Cotton Textiles	0.05	0.05	0.05	0.50	0.64	0.59	0.66	0.93	0.99	0.55	0.65
Drugs & Pharmaceuticals	0.06	0.06	0.08	0.77	0.56	0.76	0.44	1.00	1.13	0.76	0.50
Electric Machinery	0.05	0.05	0.05	0.90	0.91	0.85	0.89	1.03	1.01	0.88	0.90
Electronics	0.14	0.11	0.12	0.71	0.57	0.83	0.61	0.89	0.94	0.74	0.58
Food Products	0.05	0.06	0.07	0.75	0.64	0.84	0.53	0.93	1.14	0.78	0.60
Iron & Steel	0.46	0.36	0.29	0.88	0.76	0.99	0.97	0.89	0.80	0.89	0.78
Metal Products	0.13	0.11	0.12	0.75	0.52	0.87	0.56	0.91	0.89	0.79	0.53
Non-electric Machinery	0.16	0.12	0.14	0.84	0.89	0.99	0.97	0.86	0.93	0.85	0.90
Non-ferrous Metal	0.16	0.12	0.14	0.84	0.89	0.99	0.97	0.86	0.93	0.85	0.90
Non-metallic Mineral	0.08	0.08	0.08	0.89	0.63	0.89	0.62	1.00	1.00	0.89	0.63
Synthetic Textiles	0.09	0.08	0.11	0.68	0.87	0.84	0.74	0.90	1.09	0.76	0.81
Transport Equipment	0.06	0.10	0.16	1.10	0.95	0.96	0.91	1.12	1.12	1.08	1.02
Wood & Paper	0.08	0.08	0.09	0.76	1.06	0.87	0.93	0.95	1.06	0.83	0.98
All Industries	0.13	0.13	0.15	0.82	0.78	0.87	0.74	0.97	1.03	0.84	0.76

Sources: CMIE, Prowess (2005), GoI [CSO] (1992).

Notes: HI—Herfindahl Index; r—correlation of market shares; b—regression coefficient of share in terminal year on that in the initial year; √C(HI)—square root of the ratio of Herfindahl Index in the terminal year to the initial year; √C(HI)*r—the square root of the product of change in the Herfindahl Index and the correletion coefficient between shares relating to the two end time points.

groups taken together, there is no change in static concentration in the short period but a small increase from 0.13 to 0.15 in the long period. Comparison over the second short period, 1995 to 2001, seems important since it corresponds to the reform period. Table 3.1 shows that *HI* in 2001 was higher than in 1995 for 10 industries, lower only in one and the same in the remaining three. Thus, interestingly it is seen that in the reform period, *HI* increased in a majority of industries. Between 1989 and 1995 such a trend was not noticed. Industry-wise analysis shows, as depicted in Figure 3.1, that a high and systematic increase in the *HI* is observed in beverages and tobacco industry. An increasing trend in *HI* is also observed in the case of transport equipment and food products but from a lower base of concentration implying plausible increasing monopoly.[5]

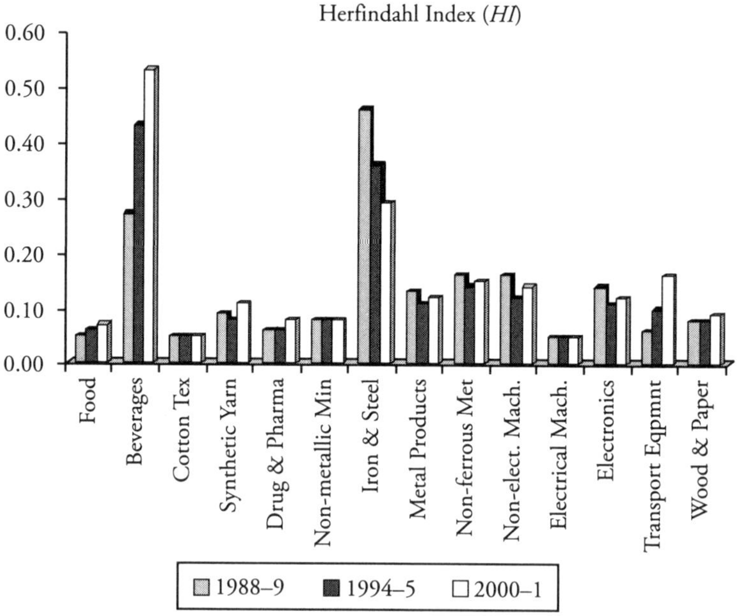

FIGURE 3.1: Herfindahl Index by Industry for Selected Years (1988–9, 1994–5, and 2000–1)

Sources: CMIE, Prowess (2005), GoI (1992).

[5] This is possible only if the industry shows stable profit rates along with increase in the concentration ratio as suggested by Grossack.

As against this, we have Iron & Steel where *HI* is systematically declining from a high level implying declining concentration. Cotton textiles, Non-metallic minerals, and Electrical machinery show stable results. The remaining seven industry groups reveal mixed trends over the short and long period. It is to be noted that a careful examination of the mixed results indicates increasing concentration in the long run in Synthetic textiles, Drugs & Pharmaceuticals, and Wood & Paper. Similarly, declining concentration is observed in Metal products, Non-ferrous metals, Non-electrical machinery, and Electronics.

How do these findings match with that of other similar studies such as Baskar (1992), Kambhampati (1996), Ramaswamy (2006), Athreya and Kapur (2006), and Bhavani and Bhanumurti (2007) among others.

Kambhampati's study relates to Structure, Conduct, Performance (SCP) Paradigm and is mainly based on data published by the Reserve Bank of India for 974 large and medium non-governmental, non-financial public limited companies, and the Annual Survey of Industries data. Using a modified *n-firm* concentration ratio, the study concludes that there is increase in concentration in 27 per cent of the industries (9 out of 33) analysed for the period 1974–85. For the period 1983–5, it is found that 48 per cent of the industries showed increased concentration. Baskar (1992) studied the level and changes in concentration for the period 1978–9 to1990–1 for 110 industries, in addition to the study of the growth of big business. Different sources of data such as Company news and notes, Assocham Parliamentary Digest, Monthly Bulletin of the Reserve Bank of India, CMIE data, and Department of Science and Technology are used for the analysis. N-firm concentration ratio is used to measure concentration. The findings of the study are that overall concentration has increased in the private corporate sector. That is, the share of the top 10 large business houses has increased from 50 per cent to 55 per cent, or 3-firm concentration increased from 63 per cent to 64 per cent.

Athreya and Kapur's (2006) study based on CMIE data for the period 1978–99 found that the concentration ratio (4-firm) rose in 22 industries out of 47 (47 per cent). Ramaswamy (2006), using CMIE data, measures changes in market concentration for the period

1993–2002 for 40 selected industry groups in the manufacturing sector using Herfindahl Index. In 21 industry groups, that is, in a little over 50 per cent of the industries considered, *HI* has increased over the period. Bhavani and Bhanumurti's study (2007) analyses changes in market structure since the early nineties based on CMIE data for the selected industries. There is a rise in concentration ratio in 38 products out of the 83 products considered (46 per cent). HI increased over the period 1994–2005. All these studies show that the percentage of industries where concentration increased ranged from 27 per cent to 50 per cent.

The above review of the studies on concentration shows that Kambhampati's study falls in the pre-reform period while that of Baskar relates to the early reform years. Athreya and Kapur's covers both the pre- and post-liberalization period. The results of these studies are therefore not strictly comparable with that of this study. Ramaswamy and Bhavani-Bhanumurti's study strictly fall in the liberalization period and are comparable with that of our study. Ramaswamy and Bhavani-Bhanumurti's results show that the percentage of industries where concentration increased for the range from 46 per cent to 50 per cent. Our study for the period 1988–9 to 2000–1 shows that concentration increased in 43 per cent of the industries which rose to 57 per cent for the period 1995–2001 (see Table 3.1). Our findings are consistent with that of Ramaswamy and Bhavani and Bhanumurti. Thus, one may conclude that most of the studies,[6] based on static indicators, suggest that concentration increased in the manufacturing sector during the post-liberalization period.

Next, we analyse the change in the market shares of the industry groups and its components for both short and long run for understanding the dynamics of competition and share cutting in Indian

[6] Using Lerner index of competition, Pant and Pattanayak (2005) conclude that price cost margins are in general high over the nineties (1989–2003) across all industries, and in most of the industries increasing over the second half of the nineties (1996–2003). Similarly, Das and Pant's (2006) study for 1989–2003 found that competition in the corporate sector has not increased during the post-liberalization period in terms of the difference between price and marginal cost.

industries. From the regression coefficients in Table 3.1 and as depicted in Figure 3.2, we observe the following:

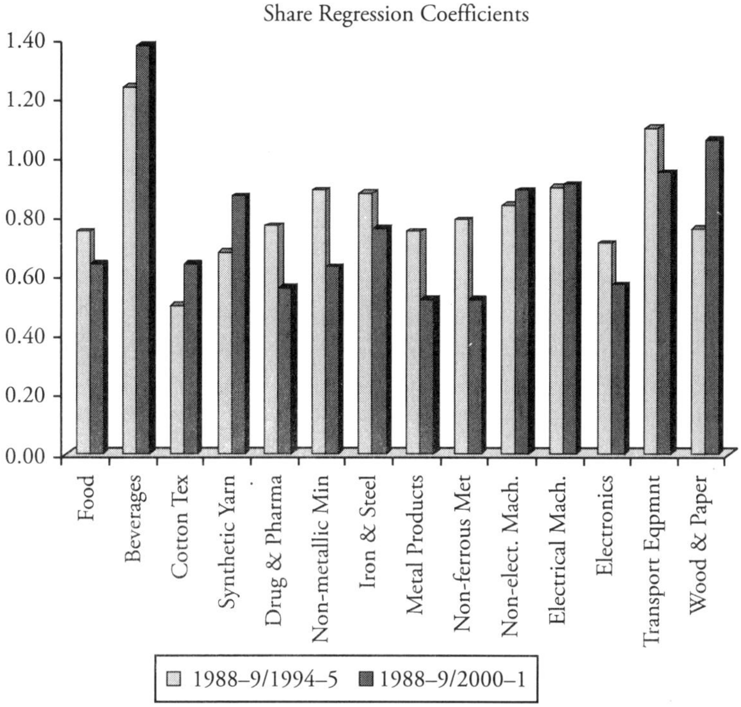

FIGURE 3.2: Share Regression Coefficient by Industry and by Period (Short Period-1988–9 to1994–5; Long Period-1988–9 to 2000–1)

Source: CMIE, Prowess (2005), GoI (1992).

In the short period, there are only two industry groups (Beverages and Tobacco and Transport Equipment) which have a value of $b>1$ indicating that the larger firms of the initial year on the average, increased their shares by 24 per cent and 10 per cent, respectively. A value of $b>1$ is also indicative of increased monopoly power. For the remaining 12 industry groups, the value of b was less than 1. This indicates that larger firms of the initial year, on an average, lost market shares, that is, they could not maintain their shares. In our sample the loss ranged from 10 per cent to 50 per cent. When we move to the long period, it is seen that in the Beverages and Tobacco industry, larger firms on an average showed an increase of

38 per cent from the initial year. That is, they showed an increase in market shares by 14 per cent from the middle year. This indicates increasing monopoly power in the long run as well. This, however, was not true in the case of Transport Equipment industry. Here although there was monopoly power in the short run, in the long run large firms on an average could not maintain market shares. Instead they lost market shares by 15 per cent.

In the short run, large firms lost market share on an average (24 per cent) but in the long run they gained 6 per cent shares from the initial year in the Wood and Paper industry. This suggests they gained monopoly power over time.

The classification of industry groups into four, as mentioned earlier by Grossack, is possible on the basis of regression coefficients taking value greater than, equal to, or less than one. However, to quote Grossack, 'The inability of large firms to maintain their market shares over a "reasonably short" period could be persuasive evidence that these firms either had no monopoly power or that any power they might have had was only for the short run. But the observed ability of the large firms to maintain or increase their shares need not necessarily indicate monopoly power since this ability could have been obtained by foregoing short-run monopoly prices and profits.'[7] The increased monopoly power is possible only if the profit rates remain the same and at the same time concentration increases. To capture the existence of monopoly power, therefore, one has to have a dynamic measure of structural change. This is given in equation 3.3 which decomposes the regression coefficient into a correlation coefficient of shares and the concentration ratio. We have adopted Grossack's classification but used the sample values of the components of market share change in equation (3.3) instead of the regression coefficients to infer the competitive process for the period.

The categorization of industry groups is based on mean value of r and $\sqrt{C(HI)}$ for all the industries in our study. If an industry's r-value is above the mean of all the industry groups, it is treated as high, otherwise low. In the case of square root of change in concentration ratio, it is high if the value is greater than the average,

[7] Grossack (1965), p. 302.

otherwise low.[8] By this classification, we have the following four groups:

r high and high $\sqrt{C(HI)}$: Group I—implying increased monopoly power;

r high and low $\sqrt{C(HI)}$: Group II—large firms as a group lost shares to small firms;

r low and high $\sqrt{C(HI)}$: Group III—large firms lost market shares to each other; and

r low and low $\sqrt{C(HI)}$: Group IV—large firms lost shares both to each other and to small firms.

Using this classification from data given in Table 3.1, we categorize the industries and interpret the results, first for the short period (Table 3.2) and subsequently for the long period in (Table 3.3). Table 3.3 also provides a concise and comparative picture of the short and the long periods.

From Table 3.2 it is clear that three industries—Beverage and Tobacco (0.94, 1.24), Non-metallic Minerals (0.89, 1.0), and Transport Equipment (0.96, 1.12) fall in Group I (high *r*, high $\sqrt{C(HI)}$) implying increased monopoly power. At the other end, we have four industries in Group IV (low *r*, low $\sqrt{C(HI)}$).

They are Food Products (0.84, 0.93), Cotton Textiles (0.59, 0.93), Synthetic Textiles (0.84, 0.90), and Electronics (0.83, 0.89) where large firms lost market shares to other large and small firms, thus indicating less mobility barriers and greater competition. In Group II (high, low), we have five industries; Iron & Steel (0.99, 0.89), Metal Products (0.87, 0.91), Non-electrical Machinery (0.99, 0.86), Wood and Paper (0.87, 0.95), and Non-ferrous metals (0.90, 0.92). In this group, large firms as a group lost shares to small firms. In the case of Group III (low, high), we have two industries—Drugs & Pharmaceuticals (0.76, 1.00) and Electrical machinery (0.85, 1.03). Here large firms lost shares to other large firms.

Monopoly and share cutting in the long period is summarized in Table 3.3 along with short period results for ease of comparison. In the long run we have four industries (Electrical Machinery, Transport

[8] This is a relative ranking of the 14 industries since it is based on averages.

Table 3.2
Industry Groups by Monopoly Power and by Share Cutting (Short Period)

Correlation (r) \ Concentration √C(HI)	High (≥ 0.97)	Low (< 0.97)
High (> 0.87)	*Group I* Beverage & Tobacco (0.94, 1.24) Non Metallic Minerals (0.89, 1.0) Transport Equipment (0.96, 1.12) Subtotal: 3	*Group II* Iron & Steel (0.99, 0.89) Metal Products (0.87, 0.91) Non-Electrical Machinery (0.99, 0.86) Non-Ferrous Metals (0.90, 0.92) Wood & Paper (0.87, 0.95) Subtotal: 5
Low (< 0.87)	*Group III* Drugs and Pharmaceuticals (0.76, 1.00) Electrical Machinery (0.85, 1.03) Subtotal: 2	*Group IV* Food Products (0.84, 0.93) Cotton Textiles (0.59, 0.93) Synthetic Textiles (0.84, 0.90) Electronics (0.83, 0.89) Subtotal: 4

Source: CMIE, Prowess (2005), GoI [CSO] (1992).
Notes: 1. The numbers in the parenthesis are the value of correlation coefficient and the square root of the ratio of Herfindahl Indices of the initial and terminal year respectively.
2. (0.97) is the mean of √C(HI) for 14 industries; 0.87 is the mean of correlation coefficient of shares of 14 industries.
3. Subtotal refers to number of industries in each group.

Equipment, Wood & Paper, and Beverage & Tobacco) falling in monopoly group that is in Group I. While Electrical Machinery and Wood & Paper have newly joined the group, Non-metallic Minerals lost its monopoly power. Two industries continued to maintain or increase their market share both in the short run and long run. They are Transport Equipment and Beverage & Tobacco. At the other extreme in Group IV compared to the short run

Table 3.3
Monopoly Power, and Share Cutting by Industry and by Period

Classification*	Industry	
	Short Period (1988–9/1994–5)	Long Period (1988–9/2000–1)
Group I (High r, High √C(HI))	*Beverages & Tobacco* *Transport Equipments* Non-Metallic Minerals	*Beverages & Tobacco* *Transport Equipments* Electrical Machinery Wood & Paper
Group II (High r, Low √C(HI))	*Iron & Steel* *Non-Electrical Machinery* Metal Products Wood & Paper Non-Ferrous Metals	*Iron & Steel* *Non-Electrical Machinery*
Group III (Low r, High √C(HI))	*Drugs & Pharmaceuticals* Electrical Machinery	*Drugs & Pharmaceuticals* Food Products Synthetic Textiles Non-Metallic Minerals
Group IV (Low r, Low √C(HI))	*Cotton Textiles, Electronics* Food Products Synthetic Textiles	*Cotton Textiles, Electronics* Metal Products Non-Ferrous Metals

Source: CMIE, Prowess (2005), GoI [CSO] (1992).
Note: *High—Above the mean of all industries in the sample.
Low—Below the mean of all industries in the sample.

period, the number of industries remained the same (4) while their composition changed. Cotton Textiles and Electronics continued to remain in the same group. Food Products and Synthetic Textiles became less competitive while Metal Products and Non-ferrous Metals became more competitive. Within Group II (high, low) fall two industries, declining from five in the short period. They are Iron & Steel and Non-electrical Machinery. In these industries concentration has declined as a result of large firms as a group losing their shares to smaller ones. In Group III, there is an increase in the number of industries from two in the short period to four in the long period. They are Food Products, Synthetic Textiles, Drugs & Pharmaceuticals, and Non-metallic Minerals. Here concentration has declined because large firms lost shares to each other indicative of oligopoly structure. Out of four, three are new entrants.

As a final test for the appropriateness of the methodology on which we have based our conclusions, following Grossack, we test for the relationship between the static index of concentration (HI [1989]) and each of the dynamic measures—*b*, *r*, and √C(HI)—by estimating simple and partial correlation coefficients. The results are given in Table 3.4. We have tested this relationship only for the long run period.

Table 3.4
Simple and Partial Correlation of *HI* (89) with *b*, *r*, and √C(HI)

Structural Change Measures	Correlation Coefficients HI (89)	
	Simple	Partial
b	0.22 (0.46)	0.15 (0.65)
r	0.44 (0.12)	–0.04 (0.91)
√C(HI)	–0.24 (0.42)	–0.21 (0.51)

Source: CMIE, Prowess (2005), GoI [CSO] (1992).
Notes: 1. Numbers in the brackets are the probability levels of significance (2-tailed).
2. HI (89)—Herfindahl Index of 1988/89; *r*—Correlation of Market Shares between initial and terminal years; *b*—Regression Coefficient of shares for initial and terminal years; √C(HI)—Square root of the ratio of Herfindahl Index for initial and terminal years.

The result shows that the static concentration measure is not strongly correlated with the dynamic measures in the statistical sense. This reaffirms that monopoly power cannot be assessed in terms of either static or dynamic indicators alone. Only by integrating the two can one assess if monopoly power has changed.

SUMMARY AND CONCLUSIONS

This chapter is an attempt to understand the vigour of competition in Indian industries for the period 1989–2001 using a balanced panel data with a model, which integrates both static and dynamic measures of concentration. The main focus of this chapter is to understand the movement of market shares among firms. Firm-level data (497 firms) for 14 industry groups are used for the study. For all industry groups taken together between 1988–9 and 1994–5, there is no change in static concentration but a small increase from 0.13 to 0.15 is observed for the period 1994–5 to 2000–1.

Comparison over the period 1995 to 2001, corresponding to the reform period shows that *HI* in 2001 was higher than in 1995 for 10 industries, lower only in one, and the same in the remaining three. Thus, interestingly it is seen that in the reform period *HI* increased in a majority of industries. Between 1989 and 1995, such a trend was not noticed. Industry-wise analysis shows a high and steady increase in the Herfindahl Index in the beverages and tobacco industry.

An increasing trend in *HI* is observed in the case of Transport Equipment, Food Products also but from a lower base implying increasing concentration. As against this, we have Iron and Steel where *HI* is steadily declining from a high level implying declining concentration. Cotton Textiles, Non-metallic Minerals, and Electrical Machinery show stable results. The remaining industry groups reveal mixed trends over the short and long period.

Next we analyse the change in the market shares of the industry groups and its components for both the short and the long run for understanding the dynamics of competition and share cutting in Indian industries. From the regression coefficients, we observe the following: In the short run, in two industry groups (Beverage and Tobacco, and Transport Equipment) the larger firms increased their shares reflecting greater monopoly power. In the remaining 12 industry groups, larger firms lost market shares. In the long period larger firms in the Beverages and Tobacco Industry could also increase shares. But this was not the case with the large firms in Transport Equipment industry—they couldn't maintain their market shares in the long period. In contrast to this, large firms in the wood and paper industry which lost shares in short run gained them in the long run, thereby gaining monopoly power.

To understand monopoly power and share cutting affecting competition, we adapt Grossack's classification by using the value of r and $\sqrt{C(HI)}$ instead of the regression coefficients. Since a value of $b > 1$ by itself cannot be considered an indication of monopoly power as noted by Grossack himself, we take high r and high $\sqrt{C(HI)}$, the two components of b as indicative of the presence of monopoly power (Group I): it may be noted that if an industry's r value is above the mean of all the industry groups, it is treated as high and if otherwise, low. In the case of change in concentration ratio, it is high if the value is greater than the average of all industry groups, otherwise low. By this classification, we have four groups. We group the industries accordingly for the short period and the long period. The major findings are the following: In the short period there are three industries—Beverage and Tobacco, Non-Metallic Minerals, and Transport Equipment with monopoly power. Where share cutting took place we had three groups. In Group II, five industries—Iron & Steel, Metal Products, Non-electrical Machinery, Wood & Paper, and Non-ferrous Metals, large firms as a group lost shares to small firms. In Group III, two industries, namely, Drugs and Pharmaceuticals and Electrical Machinery, large firms lost shares to other large firms. In Group IV, four industries included Food Products, Cotton Textiles, Synthetic Textiles, and Electronics, large firms lost market share to other large and small firms indicating greater mobility and greater competition.

As for monopoly and share cutting in the long period, we have four industries (Electrical Machinery, Transport Equipment, Wood & Paper, and Beverage & Tobacco) falling in the Monopoly group (Group I). While Electrical Machinery and Wood & Paper have newly joined the group, Non-metallic Minerals which earlier belonged to this group, lost its monopoly power. Two industries continued to maintain or increase their market share both in the short run and long run. They are Transport Equipment and Beverage and Tobacco. At the other extreme in the competitive group (Group IV), the number of industries in the group (that is, IV) remained the same both in the short and long run but their composition changed. Cotton Textiles and Electronics continued to remain in the group. Food Products and Synthetic Textiles became less competitive while Metal Products and Non-ferrous Metals became more competitive by joining the group. Within Group II there are two industry groups (reduced from five in the short period), that is, Iron & Steel and Non-electrical Machinery. In these industries concentration has declined as a result of large firms as a group losing their shares to smaller ones. In Group III there is an increase in the number of industry groups from two in the short run to four in the long run. The four industry groups are Food Products, Synthetic Textiles, Drugs & Pharmaceuticals, and Non-metallic Minerals. Here concentration declined because large firms lost shares to each other, which is indicative of oligopolistic competition. Out of this three are new entrants.

As a final test of the appropriateness of the methodology on which we have based our conclusions following Grossack, we test for the relationship between the static index of concentration (HI [1989]) and each of the dynamic measures—*b*, *r*, and $\sqrt{C(HI)}$ by estimating simple and partial correlation coefficients. We have tested this relationship only for the long run period.

The result shows that the static concentration measure is not strongly correlated with the dynamic measures. This reaffirms that monopoly power cannot be assessed in terms of either static or dynamic indicators alone. Only by integrating the two can one assess if monopoly power has changed. Thus, the study also highlights the importance of the methodology for an accurate assessment of competition. Although mobility and share cutting has been analysed, the ultimate test of monopoly power depends on the power to maintain high profit rates. It is this that reflects the state of competition. How far firms in the manufacturing sector have been successful in this, and in a competitive environment is the central issue, which needs examination. In the next chapter we therefore move to the analysis of persistence of profits and the speed with which they converge to the norm.

4

Persistence of Profit Rates

Having discussed the structural dimensions of the competitive process in earlier chapters,—we now move to the performance aspects. In this chapter we discuss the behavior of profit rates.

The chapter runs into four sections. Section 1 critically reviews the literature and states the objective of the chapter. Section 2 discusses Mueller's model of dynamic competition and the choice of the appropriate models. Section 3 gives the empirical results. Section 4, the final section, contains the summary and conclusions of the study.

ISSUES IN THE LITERATURE

The first major attempt to examine the implication of competitive behaviour using the traditional theory of firm was by Stigler.[1] He postulated the hypothesis on competition and rates of return as follows: 'If competitive environment prevails in the manufacturing sector, then investment would flow from industries with lower returns to those with higher returns'. In a world of perfect foresight and free entry of firms, this implies that the rate of return on investment will tend towards equality in all industries. In his landmark book, 'Capital and Rates of Return in Manufacturing Industries', he tested two hypotheses: (i) the average rate of return will be higher in concentrated industries compared to unconcentrated industries; and (ii) the dispersion in the rates of return among concentrated industries will be higher than that of unconcentrated industries. A

[1] Stigler (1963).

related hypothesis on the stability of the pattern of returns was also examined by correlation analysis.

However, the Stigler approach has several limitations. First, the average rate of return is taken as a proxy for the competitive rate of return in this model. But this need not necessarily be valid. Second, Stigler's model, although it checks for the stability of profit rates, does not give any idea as to how much of the profit rate is carried over to the current year from the previous year. More specifically, the analysis does not decompose profit rates into its theoretically relevant components such as the permanent (long run) component reflecting the effects of factors that remain constant over time and the transitory component reflecting the influence of short run conditions.[2] Third, the study does not give any insights into the strength of competition prevailing in the industries or the time taken for the transitory component to get eliminated. Finally, this approach to measure competition is essentially based on the static view of competition. In this view, competition is 'a state of affairs' through which resources are allocated to their optimal uses for a given set of tastes and technological opportunities.[3] The assumptions of this model and its outcomes are more suited to a stationary state, which does not prevail in the real world.

As against this, the second view of competition, originating from the works of Schumpeter (1934, 1950), is a dynamic one.[4] In this view, the market is in a flux arising from the allocation of given resources for new products and production techniques and is in disequilibrium at any moment in time unlike the first view based on equilibrium.[5] More precisely, competition here is 'a dynamic process involving innovation and adaptation, survival and failure; its outcome is a variety of products and prices that evolve in complex ways over time and are produced by a changing collection of firms'.[6] More importantly, according to the Schumpeterian view, innovations in products, processes, or marketing techniques create temporary monopolistic advantages and excess profits. This attracts

[2] Kessides (1990), p. 60.

[3] Baldwin (1998), Mueller (1990).

[4] See Mueller (ed.) (1990), p. 3.

[5] Ibid. p. 2.

[6] Geroski and Mueller (1990), p. 187.

imitators and competition will drive these profits back to normal and the process will repeat. It is this dynamic version of competition, which is therefore more appropriate for understanding competition in a liberalizing economy.

While there are several studies for other countries,[7] empirical works on India based on the dynamic view are few in number. The major studies on India are those of Vaidya (1993), Kambhampati (1995, 1996), and Glen et al. (1999, 2001, 2003). A critical review of these studies brings out the contributions and limitations of the analysis and the gaps in the literature.

We begin with Vaidya's paper. Vaidya's paper is an attempt to assess the strength of competitive forces in the Indian corporate sector and to see how it compares with that of advanced countries. A simple time-series model of firm-specific profitability developed by Geroski and Jacquemin (1988) and Geroski (1990) is used for the purpose. A balanced sample of 68 firms for the period, 1960–87, is selected from the Bombay Stock Exchange Directory for the analysis. The hypotheses tested are: (i) whether profits persist over time, (ii) whether they converge (both cross-sectionally and over time), and (iii) the speed with which excess profits converge to the norm. These are taken as indicators of how far firms are able to maintain their monopoly positions. Analysis is conducted by grouping the 68 Indian firms into six sub-samples on the basis of initial profit rates. The results for India are then compared with the results for six advanced nations—US, UK, Federal Republic of Germany, France, Canada, and Japan—as reported by Odagiri and Yamawaki (1990). Inter-firm profit differentials are found to persist in every country and the adjustment coefficients are higher in five sub-samples out of six in India than in advanced countries (as reflected in the adjustment coefficient, τ_i, greater than 0.5 for five out of six sub-samples of India where 0.5 is the upper limit of the coefficient for advanced countries). In other words, a short-run deviation from the norm persists in the Indian context for a far longer period when compared to advanced countries. Thus, while the competitive process in India does push firms' profit rates towards the norm, the process is very slow and does not succeed in

[7] Mueller (ed) (1990), Yurtoglu (2004) among others.

equalizing long-run profit rates. While only 20 per cent firms in India earn permanent (positive and negative) rents, for advanced countries it ranges from 30.4 per cent to 49.2 per cent. Inter-temporal stability in profits is observed for India and it is hoped that with the newly initiated liberalization policies, this would get reduced (stability).

The two alternative hypotheses tested by Kambhampati (1995, 1996) are whether profit rates of all industries tend towards a single economy-wide competitive profit rate (that is, a situation of zero profit differentials) or whether profit differentials are likely to persist over time due to the existence of a number of barriers to convergence. For empirical verification of the hypothesis, she uses a model, which assumes a stochastic trend in profit differentials—profit differential being defined as the excess of profits (or losses) made by an industry relative to the economy average. She then further goes on to analyse the factors underlying the observed behaviour of profit differentials. The determining factors are identified as concentration ratio, advertising–sales ratio, rate of growth of output in the industry, and cost–disadvantage ratio of not being at minimum efficient scale. A dummy variable to distinguish between public sector and private sector ownership is also used. This is tested using a two-stage procedure due to lack of time-series data for some determinants. The study is done for the period 1970–85, covers 42 Indian industries, based on the data relating to the largest public limited companies compiled by the Reserve Bank of India. Of the 42 industries analysed, 12 industries show relatively low level of persistence (20–40 per cent) of profit differentials, eight industries reveal greater than 80 per cent, and 17 industries greater than 60 per cent. Thus, the results show that there is considerable persistence of profit differentials over time as indicated by the adjustment coefficient.

It is further shown that persistence of profit differentials is greater in industries with high growth, high concentration ratio, and high strategic barriers such as advertising–sales ratio. Contrary to expectations, it is also found that there is a lower persistence of profit differentials in industries with more institutional controls.

Another major work, a cross-country study on developing economies, which includes India, is that of Glen, Singh, and Matthias (1999). This study focuses on examining the behaviour of corporate profitability and its components and measures the intensity of competition during the 1980s and 1990s for nine developing countries (Argentina, India, Jordan, South Korea, Malayasia, Mexico, Peru, Thailand, and Zimbabwe). The sample used for the analysis consists of 658 largest corporations quoted in the stock markets of the above countries. The authors begin by analysing changes in corporate profitability and its components namely, profit margin and output–capital ratio. This is done using the equilibrium model of competition, which predicts that competition will reduce excess profits and disparities and increase efficiency. These propositions are empirically verified using mean and variance tests and strengthened through a multivariate analysis. Finally, the paper concludes by examining the speed with which excess profits are eroded in developing countries using an auto-profit equation based on Mueller's model. The results are then compared with those for advanced countries available from existing studies. It is observed that capital efficiency has improved and profit margins reduced in the corporate sector in the emerging markets in the post-liberalization period. On the intensity of competition, the study concludes that the dynamics of the competitive process is no less intense in developing countries than in advanced countries. For India, the adjustment coefficient is estimated to be 0.356 for the period 1980–92.

The second study by Glen et al. (2001) is a time-series analysis of the persistence of profitability of 339 firms in seven emerging markets—India, Malaysia, Korea, Brazil, Mexico, Jordan, and Zimbabwe. While three countries (Argentina, Peru, and Thailand) have been dropped from the earlier analysis, one has been newly added, that is, Brazil. The number of companies covered is also less compared to the earlier analysis because of the non-availability of continuous data. The period of study is from the early eighties to the early nineties with slight country variations. For India, the analysis relates to the period 1982–92 and covers 40 firms. The focus is on identifying the dynamics of the competitive process by measuring the intensity of competition. Here again, following Mueller (1986, 1990), profit differential is taken as deviation of profit rates from the average profitability of all other firms in each country sample. The methodological improvement seen in this study is that they have replaced the first order model of the auto-profit equation of Mueller with a second order model, given the relatively short dimension of the data. As in the earlier study, it is found that the persistence of profit rates for emerging economies is lower than that of advanced economies. For India, the adjustment coefficient is 0.221 for the period 1982–92. This study further checks out on the plausibility of a negative relationship between persistence of profit rates and intensity of competition assumed in the studies for advanced countries. However, this proposition is not empirically verified. Instead, they quote certain studies for Korea, Japan, etc., which found that they need not be negatively related. The authors further cite other possible factors such as quality of data, exchange rate shifts, lack of inflation adjustment etc., which could affect the value of the adjustment coefficient but do not empirically verify them and leave them as areas for future research.

The third study of Glen et al. (2003) is a more rigorous and expanded analysis of the important issues discussed in the two earlier papers (Glen, Lee, and Singh 2001; Glen et al. 1999), both in terms of empirical verification and theoretical underpinnings. This study also analyses corporate profitability in seven developing countries using the methodology of persistence of profit rates, studies and compares the results with those for advanced countries. The sample consists of 339 firms relating to seven developing countries generally spanning the period 1980–95. But the studies relating to advanced countries vary vastly in their periods of analysis. The analysis shows that both short-term and long-term persistence of profitability obtained from auto-profit regression equations was lower for developing countries than that of advanced countries. To provide an explanation for the persistence of profit rates, the two components of profitability namely, profit margin and capital productivity, are analysed. This is to see if the superior profitability of large firms is either due to greater persistence of monopoly power or economic efficiency. The results show that there is more persistence of output–capital ratios than of profit margins. This is taken as compatible with the Demsetz hypothesis and the Chicago view of competition with significant caveats. This is also interpreted as indicating a slow speed of adjustment of low productivity firms to reach higher productivity levels. Another important finding is that profitability, profit margins, and output–capital ratios are all level stationary. It is also reported that the average values of adjustment coefficients for the seven countries are in the range 0.01 to 0.42 with relatively small standard errors. These results suggest that nearly all of the impact of a profitability shock dissipates within one to four years. For India, the adjustment coefficient is found to be 0.213.

The above studies tested for persistence of profit rates and tried to provide various explanations. The studies covered either the pre-liberalization period or a mix of the pre- and post-liberalization periods. The main drawback of Vaidya's study is that the sample size is very small and the larger part of the analysis (20 years, 1960–87) relates to a period when controls were still strong and the study covered only seven years of the early liberalization phase (1980–7). Hence the assessment of competition of this study largely relates to the pre-reform period.

Kambhampati's study relates to the period 1970–85, again a period when there were severe controls on prices, output, entry, etc., as in the case of Vaidya. Therefore, the results deal with the pre-reform period.

Although an attempt has been made by Glen et al. (1999) to separate 1980–92 into pre- and post- liberalization periods through the use of a time dummy, there are only three observations for the post-liberalization period as far as Indian data is concerned. This is too short a period for measuring the impact of liberalization. As for the study of Glen et al. (2001, 2003), the analysis combines the regulatory and the liberalized period. It is quite possible that some of the unexpected results contained in the studies could be attributed to the choice of the period of analysis. Further, the comparable results for the advanced countries are based on secondary studies relating to widely differing periods. Most of the studies for the advanced countries relate to the period prior to early eighties. As for the methodology employed in the studies reviewed, all of them have used the same definition of profit differentials, that is, deviation of the profit rate from the economy-wide average or sample mean. In the literature there are other definitions of profit differentials as well. The most suitable definition of the concept of profit differential to be employed could have been chosen on the basis of some statistical criteria.

One important gap in these studies is that none of them has estimated the competitive rate of profit so that the long-run component of rent which is a crucial factor affecting convergence can be assessed. Our study tries to overcome the above limitations. We choose a recent period for analysis, methodologically improve on the earlier studies by using statistical criteria for model selection, and more importantly fill a major gap in the literature by estimating the competitive rate of profit for the Indian manufacturing sector.

This chapter seeks to test the Schumpeterian thesis by empirically verifying the proposition whether the competitive process erodes excess profits and how quickly this happens. Towards this end, the objectives are the following:

(i) Assess the dynamics of competition by examining the persistence of profit rates using Mueller's methodology,
(ii) Estimate the competitive rate of profit in the manufacturing sector using Mueller's search procedure,
(iii) Decompose observed profit rate into its long run and short run components,
(iv) Test for equality of long run profit rates among firms, industry-wise, and finally,
(v) Measure the strength of competition using Cubbin-Geroski's half-life measure.

The analysis is based on the same database mentioned in Chapter 1.

DYNAMIC COMPETITION

The Mueller Model

The most significant contribution to the measurement of dynamic competition is that of Mueller.[8] This is the most commonly used model in the literature on persistence of profit rates. We also use this model for the analysis. The details of the model are given below.

[8] Mueller (1977, 1986, 1990). There are other models also such as that of Geroski and Jacquemin (1988) and Geroski (1990) for the analysis of persistence of profit rates, but only the Mueller version provides a method for the estimation of the competitive rate of return. Hence, our preference for the Mueller model.

Mueller decomposes profit rate, π into competitive rate, c, and long-run rent, r, and short-run rent, s. This would mean that profit rate of the firm i in t^{th} year, $\pi_{it,}$ can be written as:

$$\pi_{it} = c + r_i + s_{it} \tag{4.1}$$

where r_i refers to the i firm's long-run rent, c, the competitive rate prevailing in the sector, $s_{it,}$ the short-run rent of the firm i in the tth year. The transitory component, s_{it}, is assumed to have mean zero and constant variance. Mueller (1986) postulated that the short-run component of profit in equation (4.1) is inversely related to time (t) so that the limiting value of the profit function as 't' tends to infinity and can be taken as the estimate of the long-run component ($c + r_i$). More specifically,

$$s_{it} = \alpha_1 \, (1/t) + \varepsilon_{it} \tag{4.2}$$

Substituting (4.2) in (4.1), we have the profit equation,

$$\pi_{it} = c + r_i + \alpha_1 \, (1/t) + \varepsilon_{it}$$
$$= \alpha_{0i} + \alpha_1 \, (1/t) + \varepsilon_{it} \tag{4.3}$$
where $\alpha_{0i} = c + r_i$

The limit of E (π_{it}) as $t \rightarrow \infty$ is $\alpha_{0i,}$ which is taken as the long-run component of profit rate. One limitation of the model is that it exhibits an inherent bias towards convergence.[9] The second limitation of the model is that the speed of adjustment of the short-run rent cannot be assessed. To overcome these limitations, in the cross-country study on the long run behaviour of profit rates in the US, Canada, Germany, France, and UK, it is postulated that the short-run rents are inter-temporally related but converge to zero.[10]

Under this specification,

$$s_{it} = \lambda_i s_{it-1} + u_{it} \, , \; 0 < \lambda_i < 1 \tag{4.4}$$

where λ_i is the speed of convergence, the persistence with which profits differ from period by period from their long run level.[11]

[9] Kambhampati (1995), p. 354.
[10] Mueller (ed.) (1990), p. 35.
[11] Geroski and Mueller (1990), p. 189.

Multiplying (4.1) for period $t-1$ by $\lambda_{i,}$ we have

$$\lambda_i \pi_{it-1} = \lambda_i (c + r_i) + \lambda_i s_{it-1} \qquad (4.5)$$

Subtracting (4.5) from (4.1) and re-arranging the terms, we have,

$$\pi_{it} = (1 - \lambda_i)(c + r_i) + \lambda_i \pi_{it-1} + s_{it} - \lambda_i s_{it-1}$$

$$\pi_{it} = (1 - \lambda_i)(c + r_i) + \lambda_i \pi_{it-1} + u_{it} \qquad (4.6)$$

where $(1 - \lambda_i)(c + r_i) = \alpha_i$

Taking expectation of (4.6) we have,

$$E(\pi_{it}) = q_i E(\pi_{it-1}) \qquad (4.7)$$

In the long run,

$$E(\pi_{it}) = E(\pi_{it-1}) = \pi_{ip} \qquad (4.8)$$

where π_{ip} is the long run profit rate for firm i,

Substituting (4.8) in (4.7) and solving for π_{ip} we have,

$$\pi_{ip} = \alpha_i / 1 - \lambda_i \qquad (4.9)$$

where λ_i is the adjustment coefficient for firm i

A test of the hypothesis that competition drives profit rates of all firms to a common level (π_p) would be:

$H_0 : \pi_{ip} = \pi_p$ for all i against the alternative

H_a : not H_0

We next move on to model specification and measurement of variables.

Model Specification

In the literature, there are different model specifications and different definitions of profit differentials. The appropriate model and definition of profit differential to be employed has to be chosen on the basis of some statistical criteria. In this chapter profit rate is defined as the ratio of Profit after Tax plus Interest Payments to Total Assets (excluding revaluation and depreciation). This is the definition followed by Mueller and most other studies in the literature.[12] Again, following Mueller we use the accounting rate of profit and not the economic rate of profit as theory would dictate.[13] As for profit differentials, Mueller (1990, 1986) has used two variants in the estimation of equation (4.5). They are: (i) Deviations of profit rates from the sample mean (Model 1),[14] and (ii) Deviations of the profit rate from the sample mean normalized by sample mean (Model 2).[15] In addition to the above two, we consider the profit rate without any transformation as a third variant for the present analysis (Model 3). In this chapter, in addition, to the standard model AR (1), we have also tested the auto-regressive moving average model with order one—ARMA (1, 1). This will give us a total of six models to be estimated:

Model I (a), Model I (b); Model II (a), Model II (b); Model III (a), Model III (b).

Model I (a): AR (1)

$$\pi_{it} - \bar{\pi} = \alpha_0 + \lambda_i(\pi_{it} - \bar{\pi}) + u_{it};$$

where the dependent variable is the deviation from the sample mean $\bar{\pi}$ and u_{it} is the classical error term

Model I (b): ARMA (1, 1)

$$\pi_{it} - \bar{\pi} = \alpha_i + \lambda_i(\pi_{it-1} - \bar{\pi}) + u_{it} - u_{it-1}$$

where I (b) is I (a) with the error term which follows first order Auto regression.

Model II (a): AR (1)

$$\frac{\pi_{it} - \bar{\pi}}{\bar{\pi}} = \alpha_i + \lambda_i\left(\frac{\pi_{it-1} - \bar{\pi}}{\bar{\pi}}\right) + u_{it}$$

where the dependant variable is the deviation of profit rates of the ith firm from the sample mean normalized with respect to the sample mean

[12] Mueller (1990), Since most studies in the literature use this definition, for comparative reasons we also use the same.

[13] See Mueller (1990), chapter 1, Appendix for details. For this reason the referee has suggested that the term 'profit rate' may be used instead of rate of return and we have followed that.

[14] Mueller (ed.) (1990), chapter 3.

[15] Mueller (1986).

Model II (b): ARMA (1, 1)

$$\frac{\pi_{it} - \bar{\pi}}{\bar{\pi}} = \alpha_i + \lambda_i \left(\frac{\pi_{it-1} - \bar{\pi}}{\bar{\pi}} \right) + u_{it} - u_{it-1}$$

where II (b) is II (a) with the error term which follows first order Auto regression.

Model III (a) AR (1)

$$\pi_{it} = \alpha_i + \lambda_i \pi_{it-1} + u_{it}$$

Model III (b) ARMA (1,1)

$$\pi_{it} = \alpha_i + \lambda_i \pi_{it-1} + u_{it} - u_{it-1}$$

In model III (a) and (b), the profit rate is without any deviation or normalization.

We have run the regressions relating to the six models for each of the 497 firms to choose the appropriate model for our analysis. That is, to choose the model which will give the appropriate definition of profit rate/differential and the auto-regressive scheme to be used for the rest of the analysis using statistical criteria. The two most commonly used model selection criteria are the Akaike Information Criterion (AIC) and the Schwartz Bayesian Criterion[16] (SBC). Although both can be used to select the model[17] in a large sample, in small samples AIC is preferred to SBC.[18] Our sample size for certain industry groups is small and hence we opt for AIC criterion. The model selection criterion is: 'smaller the AIC value, better the fit'. As the fit of the model improves, the AIC will approach to minus infinity. The average AIC values for the six models are reported in Table 4.1. Based on the AIC values, it is seen from Table 4.1 that the best fit for our data set is model III(a), that is, the AR (1) model, the profit rates without any transformation. Hence, this profit rate is used for the rest of the analysis. The estimation of the model and its implications for competition are taken up next.

[16] Enders (2004), p. 69.

[17] Ibid. p. 107.

[18] While at the aggregate level our sample is large, at the industry-level some samples are small and the time period covered is only 13 years. Hence we use the AIC criterion.

Table 4.1
Average Akaike Information Criterion (AIC) for the Six Models
No. of Firms = 497

Average AIC	
AR (1)	ARMA (1, 1)
Model I (a) –39.38	Model 1 (b) –38.61
Model II (a) 36.36	Model II (b) 36.56
Model III (a) –39.65	Model III (b) –38.67

Calculated from auto-profit equations of 497 firms.
Source: CMIE, Prowess (2005).

EMPIRICAL RESULTS

In this section we first examine the summary results of the auto-profit equations for individual firms to understand the persistence of profit rates and the frequency distributions of the parameter estimates of λ_i, and π_{ip}, the short run and long run profit rate, respectively. Then, using Mueller's search procedure, we proceed to estimate the competitive rate of profit in the manufacturing sector from the distribution of long run profit rate. This enables the observed profit rate to be decomposed into its components—the competitive rate and the long run and short run rent. Inter- industry variations in these components are then analysed. This is followed by testing for equality of long run profit rates in each industry. The last sub-section tests for the strength of competition by estimating the half–life of the transitory component of the profit rates.

The auto-profit equations based on Model III (a) were estimated for the 497 firms using data for the years 1988–9/2000–1 to arrive at the permanent component of profit rate and the proportion of profit rate carried over from the previous year to the next (current) year and the summary results are reported in Table 4.2. It can be seen from Table 4.2 that the value of mean R^2 is 0.26.[19] This gives a good fit to the auto-regressive profit equation of the firms. This implies that the transitory component of a firm's profit rate is inter-temporally related, and would require more than a year to be eliminated. The average value of λ_i further shows that 47 per cent of the transitory component of the profit rate of the previous year is

[19] This value compares well with the results of many other studies for example, Mueller (ed.) (1990), p. 37.

carried over to the current year's profit rate. The average permanent component of the profit rate (π_{ip}) is estimated to be 9.2 per cent. This is the summary view for 497 firms. But this does not give us any idea of the distribution of these values among firms. To understand this we examine the frequency distribution of λ_i in Table 4.3 and π_{ip} in Table 4.4.

Table 4.2
Summary of Estimated Auto-profit Equations of 497 Firms

$$\pi_{it} = \alpha_i + \lambda_i \pi_{it-1} + u_{it}$$

	Mean	Standard Error*	Minimum	Maximum
$\hat{\pi}_{ip}$	0.092	2.501	–7.606	6.806
$\hat{\lambda}_i$	0.465	0.286	–0.542	4.135
R^2	0.26	—	—	—

Sources: CMIE, Prowess, (2005), GoI [CSO] (1992).
Note: *The standard error is based on Kmenta approximation[20] for ratios, $\frac{\alpha_i}{1-\check{\lambda}_i}$;

Table 4.3
Distribution of Adjustment Coefficient of Short Run Profit Rate ($\hat{\lambda}_i$) of 497 Firms

$\hat{\lambda}_i$	Frequency
Less than –1	0
Between –1 and –0.5	1
Between –0.5 and 0	50
Between 0 and 0.5	226
Between 0.5 and 1	192
Greater than 1	28
Total	497

Sources: CMIE, Prowess, (2005), GoI [CSO] (1992).

From Table 4.3, it is seen that nearly 10 per cent (51 out of 497 firms) of the firms have negative λ values and only one is statistically different from zero at 10 per cent level (one-tailed). The $\hat{\lambda}_i$ is greater than one in 28 firms, 5.6 per cent of the total sample. This would mean that altogether 15.8 per cent of the firms do not follow the specification given in equation (4.6). In other words, the model is valid only for 418 firms (84.2 per cent). Of the 418 firms, 225

[20] See Kmenta (1971), pp. 442–4.

Table 4.4
Distribution of Long Run Profit Rates ($\hat{\pi}_{ip}$)

$\hat{\pi}_{ip}$	Frequency
< 0	61
0 to 0.1	196
0.1 to 0.2	222
0.2 to 0.3	6
0.3 to 0.4	2
0.4 to 0.5	1
>0.5	9
Total	497

Sources: CMIE, Prowess, (2005), GoI [CSO] (1992).

firms had λ_i positive and significantly different from zero (at 10 per cent level one-tailed). This would mean that the relationship is significant for about 54 per cent of the valid cases studied. In other words, for 54 per cent of these firms the transitory component of profit rate is inter-temporarily related. We next examine the frequency distribution of the π_{ip} given in Table 4.4. This will give an idea as to the range in which the competitive rate will lie.

The distribution is positively skewed with concentration in two class intervals, (0 to 0.1) and (0.1 to 0.2). The maximum frequency is in the class interval (0.1 to 0.2). The table shows that 61 firms have negative long-run profits. The remaining 18 firms have a large permanent profit rate (greater than 20 per cent). Since the maximum frequency of the profit rate is concentrated between the rates, 0 and 0.20, one can infer that the competitive rate lies within this range. In order to arrive at the exact value of the competitive rate (point estimate), we use Mueller's search procedure as described below.[21]

According to Mueller, most firms in a competitive economy should either have returns on capital close to the competitive return (c) or converging on it. Thus, the number of ($\hat{\pi}_{ip}$) significantly different from c should be less than for any other arbitrarily chosen benchmark return on capital. The average of the range within which this happens is taken as the competitive rate of return. This is the search procedure of Mueller for computing the competitive rate

[21] Mueller (1990), pp. 38–9.

from the long-run profit rates. The application of this procedure to our data is discussed below.

From the estimated auto-profit equations, the permanent component of the profit rate is found to vary from –1 to +1. The competitive rate has to be located within this range. Therefore, the search procedure will start with –1 as the first benchmark value and estimate the number of firms in the sample with profit rate statistically different (at 10 per cent level of significance—two-tailed) from –1. By this criterion we have 468 firms in the first benchmark. The test is repeated by increasing each time the benchmark by 0.1. The results are given in Table 4.5.

Table 4.5
Mueller's Search Method and the Competitive Rate of Profit

Benchmark $\hat{\pi}_{ip}$*	Number of firms, with $\hat{\pi}_{ip}/SE(\hat{\pi}_{ip}) > 1.81$**
–1.0	468
...	...
0	106
0.05	17
0.1	34
0.15	71
0.2	162
...	...
0.3	350
...	...
1	468

Sources: CMIE, Prowess, (2005), GoI [CSO] (1992).
Note: * Only selected values are reported here in order to save the space.
** 1.81 is the critical value (two-tailed) at 10 per cent level.

The number of firms with different permanent profit rates decreases as the benchmark increases until it reaches the value 0.05 with 17 firms. The number of firms steadily increases thereafter. The competitive rate, as defined by Mueller (1990), is the benchmark rate in which the number of firms is the minimum. By this criterion, the competitive profit rate in the manufacturing sector is 5 per cent as is evident from Table 4.5. This implies that the average long run firm-specific rent in the manufacturing sector is 4.2 per cent (9.2 per cent –5 per cent), since the permanent profit rate is, by definition, the sum of the two components. Since the competitive rate has been now estimated, the decomposition of the observed profit rate as specified in equation (4.1) can be undertaken to bring out inter-industry variations. The results are reported in Table 4.6.

Table 4.6
Decomposition of Profit Rates by Industry

Industry	Number of Firms	Mean			
		π_{ip}	$\hat{\pi}_{ip}$	$\hat{r}_i = \hat{\pi}_{ip} - 0.05$	s_{it}
1	2	3	4	5	6=4-5
Beverage & Tobacco	14	0.088	0.147	0.097	–0.059
Cotton Textiles	51	–0.050	–0.121	–0.171	0.071
Drugs & Pharmaceuticals	30	0.136	0.156	0.106	–0.020
Electric Machinery	47	0.092	0.088	0.038	0.004
Electronics	30	0.083	0.079	0.029	0.004
Food Products	41	0.113	0.098	0.048	0.015
Iron & Steel	25	0.058	0.092	0.042	–0.034
Metal Products	22	0.081	0.083	0.033	–0.002
Non-electric Machinery	59	0.080	0.179	0.129	–0.099
Non-ferrous Metal	16	0.105	0.083	0.033	0.021
Non-metallic Mineral	48	0.111	0.110	0.060	0.000
Synthetic Textiles	22	0.063	0.025	–0.025	0.038
Transport Equipment	72	0.069	0.153	0.103	–0.084
Wood & Paper	20	0.087	0.084	0.034	0.003
All Industries	497	0.075	0.092	0.042	–0.017

Sources: CMIE, Prowess, (2005), GoI [CSO] (1992).
Note: π_{it} is observed profit rate of ith firm in t^{th} year; r_i is the long-run rent component of the ith firm; 0.05 is the estimated competitive rate of return; s_{it} is the short run rent of the ith firm in year t. The values in the table are the averages of the above across firms and/or across time.

Analysis of average observed profit rates shows that it varies across industries and is negative for Cotton Textiles (see Table 4.6). As for the others, it ranges from 0.05 for Iron and Steel (which is equal to the competitive rate) to 0.13 for Drugs and Pharmaceuticals, that is 160 per cent more than the competitive rate. Long run rent (r_i) is the highest for Non-electrical Machinery (0.129) and the least in Electronics (0.029). The differences in the long run rent reflect the advantages arising from industry-firm-specific factors. While the height of entry barriers is taken as an important industry characteristic, firms-specific factors are taken to include patent holdings, brand identification and customer loyalties, cost information asymmetries, demand inelasticity, control of and favourable access to scarce resources, favourable access to distribution channels and financing, and the learning or experience curve.[22]

Next we examine whether the long run profit rates are equalized or not across firms and/or industries and the strength of competition.

Testing for Equality of Long Run Profit Rates

The hypothesis of testing for equality of long run profit rates is equivalent to testing the equality of the long run rent component of profit rates, r_i. This is because the competitive rate (c), a constant, has been deducted from π_{ip}. Therefore, it makes no difference if one uses π_{ip} or r_i to test for the equality of long run profit rates. In this chapter we use π_{ip} for testing the equality. There are two ways in which this can be tested. First, one could test the null hypothesis of equality of the permanent profit rate for all firms as against the alternative of not equal to each other.[23]

This hypothesis imposes linear restrictions on auto-profit equations. The regression results indicate that only in 418 firms out of 497 the auto-profit equation is valid, that is the estimate of the adjustment coefficient falls between 0 and 1. Hence the testing of the equality of long run profit rates is restricted to the 418 firms.

Null Hypothesis H_0: $\alpha_1 = \alpha_2 = \dots = \alpha_{418}$ and $\lambda_1 = \lambda_2 = \dots = \lambda_{418}$

Alternate Hypothesis H_A: Not H_0

Test Statistic:

$$F = \frac{(RSS_U - RSS_R)/q}{RSS_U/(N-2n)} \sim F(q, N\text{–}2n)$$

where RSS_u is the Unrestricted Sum of Squares; RSS_r is Restricted Sum of Squares; q is the number of restrictions; N is the total number of observations and n is the number of firms in the sample.

$$\text{Fc} = \frac{\{(4.919 - 3.873)/834\}}{\{3.873/(12*418 - 2*418)\}} = 1.35$$

22 Kessides (1990), pp. 59–60.

23 Mueller (1990).

at 5 per cent significance level

$F_{0.05}$ (834,4180) = 1.09

Decision Rule

Since Fc is greater than the $F_{0.05,}$ we reject the hypothesis of equality of long run profit rate for the sample.

However, this will not give information on how many firms have equal profit rates and how many do not. To capture this, we use the second method for testing equality. In this second method, we test the equality of profit rates between two firms at a time with all possible combinations. For example, consider the case of 14 firms in the Beverages and Tobacco industry. We begin by taking firms 1 and 2 for the first test followed by firms 1 and 3, 1 and 4, ..., 1 and 14.

The total number of tests conducted will be equal to 91 which is obtained as follows: [{14(14+1)/2} – 14]. Of the 91 tests, 37 or nearly 41 per cent were found to reject the equality of permanent profit rate. The same test was repeated for all the other industries and the results are given in Table 4.7.

Table 4.7 shows that the highest number of tests confirming the equality of long run profit rates is in the Drugs and Pharmaceutical industry. In this case, the equality of permanent profit rates (PPR) is rejected only in 10 per cent of the tests. The lowest is for the Iron and Steel industry with nearly 47 per cent of the firms showing no equality of PPR. If permanent component of profit rates stands for firm-specific rent, the analysis also suggests that Viner's concept of an average firm is more relevant in the Indian manufacturing than Marshall's representative firm,[24] since in no industry is the proportion of firms with significantly different profit rates higher than 50 per cent. This has implications for the strength of competition as well. This is examined below.

[24] Baldwin (1998), p. 3. Marshall's representative firm stands for product heterogeneity while Viner's average firm implies product homogeneity. No doubt, in the real world of industry grouping, even if there is no perfect homogeneity, it could imply higher substitution possibility. This is perhaps what is seen in the Indian context.

Table 4.7
Test of Equality of Permanent Profit Rates by Industry

Industry	Number of firms	Number of tests	No. of tests with t values > 2.064*
Beverage & Tobacco	14	91	37 (40.7)
Cotton Textiles	51	1275	535 (42.0)
Drug & Pharmaceuticals	30	435	44 (10.1)
Electric Machinery	47	1081	226 (20.9)
Electronics	30	435	108 (24.8)
Food products	41	820	168 (20.5)
Iron & Steel	25	300	141 (47.0)
Metal Products	22	231	47 (20.3)
Non-electric Machinery	59	1711	615 (35.9)
Non-ferrous Metal	16	120	48 (40.0)
Non-metallic Mineral	48	1128	432 (38.3)
Synthetic Textiles	22	231	77 (33.3)
Transport Equipment	72	2556	557 (21.8)
Wood & Paper	20	190	68 (35.8)

Sources: CMIE, Prowess, (2005), GoI [CSO] (1992).
Note: Figures in parenthesis are percentage of cases in the total number of tests, which are rejected.
* 5% level of significance (two-tailed).

Strength of Competition

The main concern here is with the behaviour of the transitional part of the profit rate. Two types of analysis are attempted here. First, we estimate what proportion of the transitional component of the profit rate in the previous year is carried over to the current year and is indicative of the persistence of profit rates. According to the standard interpretation, higher the proportion carried over (λ_i), higher the persistence of profit rates and lower the competition. Second, to measure the intensity or strength of competition, one has to assess the time taken for the transitional component of rent to be wiped out. In this exercise we estimate the time taken for the transitional component of rent to be halved as suggested in Cubbin and Geroski.[25]

According to the model specification of Mueller, for estimating the proportion of the transitional component of the profit rate in the previous year being carried over to the current year, λ_i's have to be

[25] Cubbin and Geroski (1990), p. 151.

between 0 and 1. By this criterion in our sample we have only 418 firms. Hence, for the analysis of the behaviour of the transitional component and the strength of competition, the sample includes only these 418 firms. The results are given below in Table 4.8.

Table 4.8
Average Coefficient of Adjustment $\hat{\lambda}_i$ and
Half-Life Taken for the Transitional Component of Profit to be Halved

Industry	Number of Firms	$\hat{\lambda}_i$ Mean	Mean Half-life Time (in years)
Beverage & Tobacco	8	0.34	0.64
Cotton Textiles	39	0.54	1.12
Drugs & Pharmaceuticals	26	0.41	0.77
Electric Machinery	40	0.46	0.89
Electronics	28	0.44	0.85
Food Products	33	0.40	0.76
Iron & Steel	20	0.48	0.94
Metal Products	21	0.45	0.88
Non-electric Machinery	51	0.47	0.92
Non-ferrous Metal	15	0.48	0.95
Non-metallic Mineral	44	0.49	0.98
Synthetic Textiles	16	0.56	1.19
Transport Equipment	58	0.49	0.97
Wood & Paper	19	0.46	0.89
All Industries	418	0.47	0.92

Sources: CMIE, Prowess, (2005), GoI [CSO] (1992).

Comparison of $\hat{\lambda}_i$ values which indicate the proportion of profit rates carried over from the previous year to the current year across industries shows that in seven industries, only less than 47 per cent of the profits—the average for all industries—is carried over. The highest persistence of profits (56 per cent) is observed in the Synthetic Textiles Industry, and the least (34 per cent) in Beverages and Tobacco. But what is more important to understand the strength of competition within an industry and for comparison with other industries is the time taken for 1 per cent of the transitory component to reduce to its half level [26] (half-life). Although λ_i values

[26] Although theoretically it has to disappear, in actual practice this does not occur. The Schumpeterian theory of competition precludes such a possibility. Hence one has to measure the time taken for the transitory component to reduce to half, quarter or three-fourth. For further details, see Patterson (2000).

can be used to measure the strength of competition in any industry, for comparison across industries, it has to be standardized. We have followed Cubbin and Geroski's suggestion of half-life, defined as $T = \log \frac{1}{2} / \log \hat{\lambda}_i$, where $\hat{\lambda}_i$ is the short run adjustment coefficient of the ith firm, to estimate the strength of competition.[27] The results of the empirical exercise are as follows. For all industries on an average it takes 0.92 years for 1 per cent deviation of the transitional component of profit rate from the norm to reduce to 0.5 per cent, its half level. Five industries (Cotton Textiles, Iron and Steel, Non-ferrous Metal and Non-metallic Minerals, and Synthetic Textiles) take more time than the average for all industries. However, only two out of these five industries, Cotton and Synthetic Textiles, take substantially more time than the average. The highest value is for Synthetic Textiles (1.2). The lowest is for Beverages and Tobacco with 0.6 years.

We next compare our results with that of other studies. Vaidya's study for the pre-reform period, 1960–87, found that the adjustment coefficients were higher than 0.5 in five sub-samples out of six for India. Kambhampati's study for the period 1970–85 covering 42 Indian industries found 25 industries with adjustment coefficient greater than 0.6. Her period of analysis includes only a few years of the early liberalization phase and her results can be taken as reflective of the control regime. The adjustment coefficient for the above mentioned two studies is greater than our coefficient 0.47. This clearly suggests that competition has increased consequent to reforms. Besides, our adjustment coefficient is close to the value of the upper limit (0.5) of the adjustment coefficient of advanced countries, which are considered to be competitive. Needless to say, we need to go much farther to be as competitive as advanced countries.

As against these studies those of Glen et al. (1999, 2001, and 2003) estimate the adjustment coefficient as 0.356 for the period 1980–92, 0.221 for the period 1982–92, and 0.213 for the period 1980–95. Since these studies cover both the regulatory and a period of initial reforms, it is difficult to accept such exceptionally low values of the adjustment coefficients. Hence we do not consider them for comparison.

[27] Cubbin and Geroski (1990).

SUMMARY AND CONCLUSION

This chapter is an attempt to measure the dynamics of competition in Indian industry in the Schumpeterian perspective by analysing profit rates. One of the early attempts to examine the relationship between competition and rates of return was that of Stigler. Recent literature, however, has been critical of this model because of its static view of competition and stresses the need for a dynamic view of competition and its relevance in a fast changing world of innovations, technical change, etc. In the dynamic view, to understand competition as against a mere convergence of profit rates in the static model, the focus is on understanding the persistence of profit rates. This chapter empirically verifies the dynamic view of competition using firm-level data covering 497 firms in 14 industries in the Indian manufacturing sector for the period 1988–9/2000–1. To measure dynamic competition, the methodology pioneered by Mueller (based on auto-profit equation) and commonly used in persistence of profit rates studies is employed. We have followed Cubbin and Geroski for measuring the strength of competition.

The major findings from the chapter are the following: The average explanatory power of the auto-profit equations is 26 per cent, which is a good fit. Implicit in this finding is that a certain proportion of the transitional component of profit rate from the previous year is carried over to the next year. The average proportion carried over, as measured by the mean of the λ values is 47 per cent. The average permanent rate of return is estimated to be 9.2 per cent. This is decomposed into the competitive rate and the long run firm-specific rent. Using Mueller's search procedure, the competitive rate of profit for all industries is estimated to be 5 per cent. This gives the average long run firm specific rent as 4.2 per cent (that is, 9.2 per cent –5 per cent). It is also seen that the observed average profit rate for all industries is 7.5 per cent and is about 50 per cent higher than the competitive rate. These are the aggregate results.

Inter-industry analysis shows that in four out of the 14 industries (Food Products, Non-ferrous Metals, Non-metallic Minerals, and Drugs and Pharmaceuticals), the observed average profit rate is 100 per cent higher than the competitive rate or even more. In

Cotton Textiles alone it is below the competitive rate. Comparison of l values across industries shows that in seven industries, the proportion of short run profits carried over is less than the average for all industries (47 per cent). The highest carry over of profits is observed in the Synthetic Textiles (56 per cent) and the lowest in Beverage and Tobacco (34 per cent). The strength of competition within and across industries is estimated as the time taken for a unit change in the transitory component to reduce to its half level as suggested by Cubbin and Geroski. The results show that for all industries, on an average, it takes 0.9 years for convergence. But there are industry variations; the longest time is taken by Synthetic Textiles (1.2 years) and the shortest by Beverage and Tobacco, that is, 0.6 years.

To sum up, it is seen that competition in the Indian manufacturing sector has increased in the post-liberalization period when compared to the results of Vaidya and Kambhampati. It is also seen that the adjustment coefficient of this study (0.47) is close to the upper limit (0.5) of the adjustment coefficient of developed countries, which are assumed to be competitive. But we have to go much farther.

5

From Domestic Competition to Foreign Trade Performance

We have examined the implications of the Schumpeterian theory for the behaviour of profit rates in the previous chapter. Now we move to examine its implications for another dimension of performance namely, that of foreign trade. To recapitulate, the Schumpeterian process, through innovation, imitation, etc., creates market imperfections via increasing returns to scale (Bhaduri 2007). This increasing return to scale forms the basis for the 'new trade theory' put forth by Helpman and Krugman (1985, 1989). The major prediction of this theory is that domestic market structure is an important determinant of trade performance. The main contribution of this new trade theory lies in combining Ricardo's theory of comparative advantage with that of Adam Smith's theory of division of labour and specialization. With this was achieved the integration of the theories on trade and industrial organization in a single framework and domestic market structure assumed a significant place in trade analysis.

These theoretical developments also produced a rich array of models predicting the volume, pattern, and composition of trade (Krugman 1994). However, empirical verifications of these models are very few and mostly confined to the developed countries at the neglect of smaller economies and those at various stages of development. A critical examination of these studies reveals that the relationship between market structure and trade has been analysed assuming different causalities. However, there are very few studies testing for the causality running from domestic market structure to trade. Such causality is particularly important to our analysis since, to quote White, 'a firm with market power will face different incentives and behave differently with respect to these trade flows than would a group of competitors'.[1] In the context of an economy in transition from a controlled regime to a liberalized one, this approach seems the most appropriate one. This chapter is an attempt to fill the above gaps.

The chapter is organized into five sections. Section 1 deals with the issues in the literature and defines the scope of the chapter. Section 2 assesses the state of competition in the Indian manufacturing sector using the three independent dynamic measures. Section 3 provides an analysis of the trade data. Section 4 specifies the model and tests the relationship between domestic competition and foreign trade performance. Section 5 gives the conclusions.

ISSUES IN THE LITERATURE

The earliest theoretical work assuming a causality running from domestic market structure to foreign trade is that of White (1974). He clearly established that market structure does indeed influence trade flows. While the predictions relating to imports are clear cut, those relating to exports are ambiguous. In this analysis of the relationship between market structure and trade performance, two extremes of market structure—perfect competition and monopoly, have been considered. A whole range of structures in between which could prevail in the real world have been ignored.

It is in the major theoretical work of Helpman and Krugman (1985) that imperfect market conditions and increasing returns came to the fore as factors affecting trade. The emphasis was on explaining the trade that took place under conditions not conforming to traditional trade theory. Trade was explained in terms of the Smithonian concept of division of labour and specialization and Ricardo's theory of comparative advantage got subsumed in it. As stated earlier, this framework/approach successfully brought about an integration of trade theory with industrial organization theory and market structure gained predominance although no specific causality was assumed.

[1] White (1974), p. 1013.

Another major approach/theory, which again emphasizes the importance of domestic market structure in determining trade, is that of Porter (1990, 1998). In the place of the principle of comparative advantage, he develops an exhaustive theory of competitive advantage. According to Porter (1998), 'National prosperity is created, not inherited. It does not grow out of a country's natural endowments, its labour pool, its interest rates, or its currency's value as classical economics insists. A nation's competitiveness depends on the capacity of its industry to innovate and upgrade. Companies gain advantage against the world's best competitors because of pressure and challenge. They benefit from having strong domestic rivals, aggressive home-based suppliers, and demanding local customers'. He substantiates his theory with various country experiences. The theoretical foundations of Porter's theory of competitive advantage can be traced back to, what Schumpeter as early as 1942 called, 'the creative process of destruction or the dynamic view of competition'. Porter's contribution lies in linking this view of competition with trade performance. Domestic rivalry forms the centrepiece of his analytical construct (Sakakibara and Porter 2001).

Some major empirical studies in the tradition of White are that of Pagoulatos and Sorenson (1976), Pickering and Sheldon (1984), Yamawaki and David (1988), Nolle (1991), and Sakakibara and Porter (2001). A critical review of these papers is given below.

The Pagoulatos and Sorenson tests for the impact of market power on industry exports and imports for the US manufacturing sector for the year 1965 for a sample of 88 industries and two sub-samples consisting of 50 exporting and 38 import competing industries using multiple regression analysis. The dependent variables were the deflated values of total US exports to the rest of the world as a percentage of domestic value of shipments and total US imports as a percentage of domestic value of shipments. The independent variables used for the analysis related to domestic market power and industry characteristics. Two measures of market power were used—the weighted concentration ratio (weight being the industry value of shipments) and an employment entropy measure. The elements of industrial structure were proxied by economies of scale, product differentiation, research and development effort, and mean distance shipped. The empirical analysis gives the following results. Domestic market structure is an important factor in influencing an industry's export and import competing performance, particularly in industries protected from foreign competition. Both exports and imports were found positively related to domestic market (measured by seller concentration or entropy) and the relationship was statistically significant. The analysis is carried out in a static framework and with reference to both protected and unprotected industries.

Another major work in this area is that of Pickering and Sheldon (1984), focusing on the period 1970–7 and for 97 British industries. The data are taken from the UK Census of production series and the Overseas Trade Statistics. They test the relationship between domestic concentration and international trade performance. The assumption underlying this is that efficient firms export more and resist imports. On the other hand, monopolistic firms will be characterized by high prices, restricted output, X-inefficiency, lack of dynamism in product, and process innovation. They will also not perform well in relation to export and import substitution. In this study both exports and imports are treated as indicators of performance. Four measures of trade are used. A measure of trade involvement (TI) is calculated as exports+imports/level of domestic output—export performance is defined as the ratio of exports to gross output, import penetration is defined as the ratio of imports to all home market sales where domestic sales are defined as domestic output less exports+imports, and net trade performance is defined as (exports–imports/exports+imports). Five firm concentration ratios are used as a proxy for market structure.

The relationship is tested using OLS regression for the 97 industries, and for three subsets based on the degree of their involvement in trade. Both the level and change in trade performance are tested. Major findings from the testing of the static relationship are that more concentrated industries are likely to be better export performers but weaker import performers. The results regarding net trade are ambiguous. When change in market structure and trade performance was considered, it was found that increasing concentration (1963–71) was associated with declining exports and increasing imports (1971–7, lagged effect). In the case of net trade performance, the evidence suggested that increasing concentration (1963–71) was closely associated with a decline in net trade performance (1971–7). That is, previous concentration increases were associated with a subsequent worsening of international trade performance. One main point that is emphasized here is that it is important to recognize that international trade is an element of an industry's performance and not merely a structural dimension. The main lacuna in this study is that although it recognizes the multidimensional nature of industrial structure, it uses only the concentration ratio as a proxy to measure market structure.

Yamawaki and David (1988) examined the impact of oligopoly market structure with product differentiation on trade performance between US and Japan. The analysis is limited to US imports from Japan assuming that domestic and foreign firms engage in an oligopoly game with Cournot behaviour. In such a game of differentiated oligopoly, the import share depends on the previous commitments of both domestic and foreign firms on certain strategic variables such as product differentiation, research and development (R&D), and tangible investment. This model is estimated using a sample of 24, three-digit import competing US industries, for the year 1977. The major conclusion is that relative expenditures on the strategic variables mentioned above and the market structure explain the trade between the two countries. The limitation of this chapter is the assumption of uniform Cournot behaviour across all the industries involved in trade.

In his article, Nolle (1991), with a view to re-examine and extend the existing theories on trade and industrial organization, empirically tests the impact of domestic market structure on trade performance using a simultaneous structural equation model. Four equations were used for the estimation: (i) import share equation, (ii) export share equation, (iii) concentration equation, and (iv) profitability equation. The specification of import share equation includes, in addition to concentration: (i) exogenous industrial organization variables such as economies of scale, product differentiation, and profitability; (ii) comparative advantage variables like human capital intensity, capital-labour ratio, research and development intensity; (iii) trade barriers variables—US tariff rates and non-tariff barriers; and (iv) the transportation costs—a regional industry dummy variable based on the distance of the plant of origin from where most of the output of the industry is shipped. The difference in the specification of the export share equation from the import share equation is that profitability is excluded and both domestic tariff and non-tariff rates are replaced by its foreign counterparts. All the other variables remain the same as in the import share equation. The concentration equation contains the variables import share, export share, economies of scale, product differentiation, R&D intensity, capital cost requirement of entry, growth rate of demand in the market, and regional dummy to capture the effect of whether industry is localized or not. Finally, the profitability equation depends on import share, export share, concentration, economies of scale, product differentiation, R&D intensity, growth rate of demand, and capital-output ratio. The model is estimated by three-stage least squares method using data for 122 four-digit level US manufacturing industries for the year 1972.

The major results are: (i) concentration exerts a negative effect on export share; (ii) export share and profit rate are positively related; and (iii) concentration has no relation with import share or profitability. The message is very powerful, that is, anti-trust policy is essential for international competitiveness of domestic economy. It is important to note that the measure of competition used here is a static one and assumes simultaneity between domestic market and trade performance.

Sakakibara and Porter (2001) examined the impact of domestic competition on international trade performance. Two models are considered: a market share instability model and a trade performance model. We confine our discussion to the latter model which is more relevant to our present study. In this model, the export share (Japanese exports as a percentage of world exports) is specified as a function of domestic competition, factor endowments, protection of domestic market, scale economies, strategic variables, cartels, and import share. Factor endowment effects are measured by relative shares of unskilled labour, physical capital, and human capital in value added. Protection of domestic market is measured in terms of tariff and non-tariff barriers. Two measures are used to indicate scale economies: the scale index and the minimum efficient scale index. Strategic variables are proxied by R&D intensity, and a variable that interacts R&D intensity and market share instability. Other variables are cartels measured using a dummy variable and the industry's share of world imports. The model is estimated for 77 products (46 industrial goods and 31 consumer goods) belonging to five-to-six-digit level Standard Industrial Classification (SIC) Japanese industries for the period 1973–90. Regressions are estimated using ordinary least squares method.

The multiple regression analysis indicates that market share instability is positively related to export share and trade protection has a negative effect on export share. The explanatory power of the factor endowments' variables in determining world export share is modest. Scale factor is also not significant. When two-stage least square estimation was used to test for simultaneity, the results were the same as that in the OLS regression. This finding also indicates that a casuality running from market structure to export performance is the valid one to be used in such types of analysis.

To summarize from the above review, it is clear that there is no unanimity of findings from these studies on the relationship between domestic market structure and trade performance. On the empirical side, in most studies on the relationship between domestic market structure and trade, the industry concentration ratio or the market instability index is used to measure the extent of competition. Most of the studies use indicators that are static in nature and capture only a single dimension of competition. It is also observed from the models used in the literature for testing the relationship between competition and trade performance, that in addition to an index of competition, several other variables identified in the trade literature as having an impact on export performance are included as independent variables in the specification. These variables are factor endowments, protection of the domestic market, scale economies, R&D, and other variables to mention a few. They are incorporated on the ground that competition is not the only determinant of trade performance. It is quite possible that there may be other variables as well which cannot be measured/captured, that is, latent variables such as potential threat, entry barriers, etc., which have an impact on trade performance and are ignored in these studies. Again it is observed that some studies assume a particular market structure for all the products which may not be valid in reality.

A review of Indian studies[2] shows that while there are studies testing the impact of trade liberalization on profit mark-ups, productivity, etc., there is no study which explored a causality running from domestic market structure to international trade. This is a major gap in the literature. Testing the relationship using such causality is particularly important when policy is specifically aimed at increasing competition and improving trade performance, more so in the context of India becoming a member of the WTO. Hence this chapter is an attempt to overcome the limitations of previous studies and to fill the gaps in the literature by using more appropriate methodologies, taking into consideration the theoretical developments.

Scope of the Chapter

We assess the impact of domestic competition on growth of international trade. In contrast to the earlier studies in the literature, it uses multidimensional dynamic measures for assessing competition. Since India's share in total world trade is only around 1 per cent, the wider hypothesis of domestic competition and international trade performance tested in the literature cannot be verified in the Indian context. The chapter therefore tests for the empirical validity of the relationship between domestic competition and trade performance in Indian manufacturing industries for the period 1988–9/2000–1 using firm-level data covering 14 major industries used in the earlier chapters.

MEASUREMENT AND ASSESSMENT OF COMPETITION

In the review of the literature, it was observed that competition was measured in terms of a single indicator and static measures were used for this purpose. It is also widely accepted that competition is multidimensional and dynamic in nature and ideally competition should be measured taking into account these features (Scherer 1973, Shepherd 1982, Mueller 1990, and Lall 2001). This being so, empirical measurement of the intensity of competition, which has always been problematic, has become all the more complex. In

[2] Krishna and Mitra (1998), Pant and Pattanayak (2005), Das and Pant (2006), Virmani (2006), Athreya and Kapur (2006) among others.

this chapter we try to improve upon earlier studies by considering three new dynamic indices developed in the earlier chapters, which capture different dimensions of competition. The first is the mobility index,[3] a measure of the mixing and reordering that takes place among firms. The second is the SD index (or the regression coefficient *b*), which integrates static and dynamic measures of concentration and reveals the pattern of share cutting among firms.[4] The third an index based on the persistency of profit approach, primarily aims at capturing the speed of adjustment or the time taken for abnormal profits to be reduced/eroded[5] to a normal level.

Assessing Competition in Terms of Different Indicators

Although we have attempted to assess competition according to the above three measures capturing different dimensions of competition in chapters 2, 3, and 4, it is important to ascertain if the classification of industries as more/less competitive is the same by the three indicators. Provided below in Table 5.1 is a brief summary of the state of competition as depicted by the three dynamic measures of competition. We make a comparison of competitive industries by the three indicators.

The intensity of competition is interpreted in terms of above/below average values of each indicator for all industries. In the case of IS index and speed of adjustment, higher the value above the average, higher the competition. In the case of SD index, lower the value than the average, higher the competition. The starred (*) values give the more competitive industries by each criterion. By the ISI criterion, we have seven industries out of 14, by the speed of adjustment criterion it is again seven industries and by SD index we have eight industries. Thus, by the three indicators individually considered, 50 per cent of the manufacturing sector is competitive. However, it can be seen from the table that an industry can be competitive in terms of one criterion but need not necessarily be so

[3] Pushpangadan and Shanta (2006) and Chapter 2 in the book.

[4] Pushpangadan and Shanta (2005) and Chapter 3 in the book.

[5] Chapter 4 in the book.

Table 5.1
Three Competition Indices by Industry

Industry	IS index	Speed of Adjustment	SD Index
Beverage & Tobacco	0.002	0.66*	1.38
Cotton Textiles	0.003	0.46	0.64*
Drugs & Pharmaceuticals	0.021***	0.59***	0.56***
Electric Machinery	0.04*	0.54*	0.91
Electronics	0.037***	0.56***	0.57***
Food Products	0.017	0.60*	0.64 *
Iron & Steel	0.003	0.52	0.76 *
Metal Products	0.042***	0.55***	0.52 ***
Non-electric Machinery	0.0022	0.53	0.89
Non-ferrous Metal	0.0234*	0.52	0.52*
Non-metallic Mineral	0.0202*	0.51	0.63 *
Synthetic Textiles	0.0167	0.44	0.87
Transport Equipment	0.009	0.51	0.95
Wood & Paper	0.0186*	0.54*	1.06
All Industries average	0.0182	0.53	0.78

Sources: CMIE, Prowess, (2005); IS index, Table 2.3 col. 3; SD index, Table 3.1 col. 5; Speed of adjustment (1–mean λ_i) estimated from Table 4.8.
Notes: *Competition by the specified criterion.
***Competition by all the criteria.
In this table the IS index used relates to the terminal year (1999/2000).[6]

in terms of another criterion. By all three criteria, we have only three industries (21 per cent) which are competitive (*** and highlighted). They are Drugs & Pharmaceuticals, Electronics, and Metal Products.[7] In terms of value added, these industries account for about 19 per cent of the total value added of the sample/manufacturing sector (see Table 5.1).

It is important to note that the average value of the three different indices is taken as the demarcating line to distinguish between competitive and non-competitive industries. This is definitely arbitrary. A more accurate test to identify the most competitive

[6] Since the initial and terminal indices are highly correlated, it makes no difference which one we choose.

[7] Using the same data, Krishna and Mitra (1998) found that three industries, that is non-electrical, transport equipment, and electronics are competitive in terms of decline in mark-up behaviour (price marginal cost mark-up). Out of these three industries only one, that is, electronics is found to be competitive according to our multidimensional indices.

and the least competitive by the three indicators is therefore necessary. One way of resolving this is to go for Borda ranking.[8] The method is as follows. All the industries are ranked according to the three different indicators. In the case of speed of adjustment and ISI, the most competitive (the highest value) is given rank 1 and the next highest rank 2, etc. (descending order of competition). In the case of SD index, the least value is given rank 1 which corresponds to the most competitive industry. The ranks of each industry by the three indicators are added up to calculate the Borda ranks.[9] The least value obtained by summing the three ranks is given the first rank and taken to be the most competitive industry (see Table 5.2).

Using this criterion, we can derive two subsets from the sample of 14 industries. The first three ranks may be treated as the most competitive industries, and those with the last three ranks as the least competitive. By this criterion the three industries, that is, Metal Products, Drugs & Pharmaceuticals and Electronics (*) are the most competitive and Cotton Textiles, Non-electrical Machinery, Synthetic Textiles, and Transport Equipment (**) are the least competitive. It is interesting to note that we get the same three industries as competitive by the Borda criterion and the earlier average criterion.

Now how does domestic competition affect trade performance? Before examining this relationship, we try to get a broad overview of the trade performance in general of the companies in the sample. It is important to note that since July 1991, the Government of India embarked on a programme of substantial economic reforms involving the removal of licensing and other non-tariff barriers on all imports of intermediate and capital goods and significant reductions in tariffs on imports.[10] This analysis is therefore in the context of trade liberalization.

[8] For details and an application of Borda ranking, see QizilBash (2002), p. 767.

[9] When the sums obtained in this manner are the same for two industries, the tie is resolved by the method suggested by Yule and Kendal (1965).

[10] For details see Krishna and Mitra (1998), p. 449 and Virmani (2006) among others.

Table 5.2
Borda Rankings of Industries

Industry	IS Index	Speed of Adjustment	SD Index	Total of the Ranks	Borda Rank
Beverage & Tobacco	0.002 (14)	0.66 (1)	1.38 (14)	29	9.5
Cotton Textiles	0.003 (11.5)	0.46 (13)	0.64 (6.5)	31	11.5**
Drugs & Pharmaceuticals	0.021 (5)	0.59 (3)	0.56 (3)	11	2.5*
Electric Machinery	0.04 (2)	0.54 (6.5)	0.91 (11)	19.5	6
Electronics	0.037 (3)	0.56 (4)	0.57 (4)	11	2.5*
Food Products	0.017 (8)	0.6 (2)	0.64 (6.5)	16.5	5
Iron & Steel	0.003 (11.5)	0.52 (9.5)	0.76 (8)	29	9.5
Metal Products	0.042 (1)	0.55 (5)	0.52 (1.5)	7.5	1*
Non-electric Machinery	0.0022 (13)	0.53 (8)	0.89 (10)	31	11.5**
Non-ferrous Metal	0.0234 (4)	0.52 (9.5)	0.52 (1.5)	15	4
Non-metallic Mineral	0.0202 (6)	0.51 (10.5)	0.63 (5)	21.5	7
Synthetic Textiles	0.0167 (9)	0.44 (14)	0.87(9)	32	13**
Transport Equipment	0.009 (10)	0.51(10.5)	0.95 (12)	32.5	14**
Wood & Paper	0.0186 (7)	0.54 (6.5)	1.06 (13)	26.5	8

Source: Table 5.1; 1 = *Most Competitive*.
Notes: * Most Competitive; **Least Competitive.

TRADE PERFORMANCE

In this section we first discuss the different measures of trade performance used in the literature and then move to assess the trade performance of our sample firms. Following Pagoulatos and Sorenson (1976) and Pickering and Sheldon (1984), the most commonly used indicators of international trade performance are used in this analysis. They are trade involvement (TI) defined as (exports+ imports)/value of output, export intensity defined as exports/value of output; import penetration is defined as imports/(value of output+imports-exports), and net trade performance (NTP) defined as (export–imports)/(exports+imports). These ratios have been calculated for the beginning triennium (1988–91) and ending triennium (1998–2001), and averaged across firms for each of the fourteen industries in the sample and for all firms taken together. The results are given in Table 5.3.

From Table 5.3, it is seen that for all industries, on an average, there is an increase in export intensity, import penetration and trade involvement, and a decrease in the net trade performance ratios. It may be noted that the value of the NTP index can range between +1 and –1 depending on whether the industry is a net exporter or net importer, respectively. Our table shows that although we are still net importers, the NTP index has increased over time from –40 per cent to –13 per cent, suggesting that either our exports have increased or imports declined. Our table shows that both export and import intensity have increased, but the former more than the latter. Hence the increase in the NTP index is due to the faster growth of exports.

Industry-wise analysis of export intensity shows that seven out of the fourteen industries show above average growth in export intensity (that is, more than 125 per cent). As for import intensity, nine industries showed above average growth (28.2 per cent). Thus to reiterate, although on an average we are still net importers, the NTP index has declined substantially by almost 68 per cent. It is interesting to note that three out of the 14 industries, which were initially net importers, have become net exporters, and seven net importers have reduced their import intensities. Two others which were initially net exporters have become net importers, and the remaining two maintained their position.

Table 5.3

Trade Performance Measures by Industry, 1988–9 to 2000–1

Industry		Export Intensity			Import Penetration			NTP			TI		
	No. of firms	trie_ 1988–91	trie_ 1998–01	Change in %	trie_ 1988–91	trie_ 1998–01	Change in %	trie_ 1988–91	trie_ 1998–01	Change in %	trie_ 1988–91	trie_ 1998–01	Change in %
Beverage & Tobacco	14	0.123	0.131	6.522	0.027	0.087	226.831	0.655	0.229	–65.00	0.147	0.213	45.583
Cotton Textiles	51	0.074	0.286	285.488	0.035	0.118	234.712	0.370	0.501	35.18	0.108	0.381	253.358
Drug & Pharmaceuticals	30	0.079	0.189	140.391	0.099	0.167	68.813	–0.144	0.075	–152.44	0.180	0.351	95.645
Electrical Machinery	47	0.051	0.092	81.377	0.098	0.117	19.701	–0.342	–0.136	–60.37	0.154	0.213	38.225
Electronics	30	0.027	0.127	363.169	0.127	0.181	42.212	–0.677	–0.208	–69.35	0.170	0.321	89.152
Food Products	41	0.066	0.089	34.070	0.022	0.105	371.169	0.512	–0.091	–117.80	0.088	0.196	124.208
Iron & Steel	25	0.029	0.096	228.102	0.102	0.132	29.234	–0.583	–0.183	–68.56	0.139	0.233	67.050
Metal Products	22	0.048	0.288	506.866	0.058	0.099	70.927	–0.097	0.567	–685.60	0.106	0.367	246.758
Non-electric Machinery	59	0.043	0.066	53.599	0.144	0.121	–15.891	–0.578	–0.324	–43.99	0.204	0.195	–4.535
Non-ferrous Metals	16	0.131	0.151	14.996	0.121	0.181	49.730	0.037	–0.116	–412.52	0.251	0.339	34.973
Non-metallic Minerals	48	0.032	0.070	120.812	0.066	0.094	42.195	–0.376	–0.157	–58.13	0.100	0.167	66.138
Synthetic Textiles	22	0.018	0.089	387.145	0.128	0.057	–55.049	–0.776	0.230	–129.67	0.162	0.145	–10.830
Transport equipment	72	0.041	0.063	56.419	0.114	0.139	21.276	–0.505	–0.408	–19.12	0.165	0.214	30.223
Wood & Paper	20	0.005	0.047	770.414	0.096	0.112	17.183	–0.889	–0.445	–49.93	0.112	0.168	50.338
ALL Firms	497	0.047	0.106	124.214	0.102	0.132	28.995	–0.398	–0.127	–68.02	0.156	0.242	55.105

Sources: CMIE, Prowess, (2005), GoI [CSO] (1992).

Note: Export Intensity= Exports/value of output.

Import penetration =Imports/(value of output+imports –exports) .

NTP – Net Trade Performance ={(Exports–imports)/(export+imports)}, The values of this index will range in between +1 and –1 depending on whether the industry is a Net Exporter and Net importer, TI – Trade Involvement = Exports+imports /value of output.

trie: triennium.

Consequent to trade liberalization, trade involvement has increased over time by 55 per cent, all industries taken together. Above average involvement (in terms of per cent change) is observed in seven industries. In two industries alone there has been a decline. The remaining five have below average trade involvement (in terms of per cent change). We next proceed to examine the relationship between trade performance and competition.

COMPETITION AND TRADE PERFORMANCE

In this section what is attempted is to test whether domestic competition measured in terms of different indices and trade performances are related. Now the question is: Should all the three indicators namely the IS index, the SD index, and the persistence of profit index (PP index which is taken as $1-\lambda_i$, the adjustment coefficient in the auto-profit equation) each capture a different dimension of competition for testing the relationship. This would depend very much on whether the three indicators are correlated with each other. If the three indicators are independent, then all the three will have to be used. On the other hand if they are related, it would suffice to use anyone of them. This is ascertained through a correlation analysis among the three indices. The results are given in the Table 5.4.

Table 5.4
Correlation between Indicators of Domestic Competition

	Mobility (Ijiri-Simon) Index	SD (static and dynamic) Index	PP Index (speed of adjustment $1-\lambda$)
Mobility Index	1.00	–0.45*	0.07
SD Index	–0.45*	1.00	0.29
PP Index ($1-\lambda$)	0.07	0.29	1.00

Source: CMIE Prowess, (2005).
Note: *Significant at 10 per cent level.

Table 5.4 shows that among the three indicators, only the mobility index (ISI) and the SD index are related while the speed of adjustment index is independent. This suggests that only two indicators (ISI or SD index and PP Index) need be considered for testing the relationship between competition and trade performance.

We prefer to use the IS index and the PP index for our analysis. By these two independent indicators which capture different dimensions of competition, we are also to assess what is the state of competition in the Indian manufacturing sector.

The Model

Two relationships are tested: (i) The relationship between domestic competition and export growth and (ii) the relationship between domestic competition and imports growth. These relationships are tested for all industries with respect to the two indicators of competition and with and without interaction term.

Model Specification:

(a) $GM_i = \alpha_0 + \alpha_1 IS_i + \alpha_2 SA_i + \varepsilon_i$

$GX_j = \alpha_0 + \alpha_1 IS_j + \alpha_2 SA_j + \varepsilon_j$

(b) $GM_i = \alpha_0 + \alpha_1 IS_i + \alpha_2 SA_i + \alpha_3 SA_i {*}IS_i + \varepsilon_i$

$GX_j = \alpha_0 + \alpha_1 IS_j + \alpha_2 SA_j + \alpha_3 SA_j {*}IS_j + \varepsilon_j$

where,

GX is the growth of exports,
GM is the growth of imports,
**IS is* the Ijri-Simon Index,
SA is the Speed of Adjustment, and
i refers to importing firms and j to exporting firms
ε is the random error term

We would like to emphasize that the above specification does not include the standard variables that influence trade performance such as factor endowments, R&D expenditure, product differentiation/advertising intensity, economies of scale, among others as employed in the previous studies.[11] In all these studies, several latent and unmeasurable variables such as potential threat of entry etc., are however, excluded. Our omission of the above mentioned measurable variables in the specification may be criticized as 'an omitted variable problem' and one which could bias the results. This, however, is not correct. The problem is taken care of in another way. It is true that such variables are not explicitly

[11] For details, see review of literature in section 1 of this chapter.

included in the specification. But by using an autoregression specification, all the above measurable as well as latent variables are implicitly captured in the model. It is important to note that this is because the factors affecting the PP index (speed of adjustment) are identified[12] as almost the same variables used in the earlier specifications in the literature as industry characteristics/strategic variables, etc. According to Kessides, factors affecting adjustment coefficients are number of operating firms, levels of concentration, rapid demand growth, economies of scale, large sunk outlays, large capital requirements, and advertising expenditures. Thus, our model specification is more inclusive than the previous models, since it captures both measurable and latent variables. Again by explicitly using a model from industrial organization theory (PP studies) to explain trade performance, an integration of industrial theory and trade theory is also achieved.

The Data and Variables

While the same sample of firms used in the previous chapters is used for analysing trade statistics and covers 497 firms, for the regression analysis only a sub-sample of this is used. The basis of selection of this sub-sample is given below. In order to analyse the effect of competition on trade performance it is important to distinguish between four categories of firms: those which export only, those which import only, firms which export and import and which neither export nor import (that is, those which cater to the domestic market). However, it is observed from the data that all firms are not involved in trade activities, and for all 13 years. Therefore, a sub-sample of firms which were involved in trade for all 13 years has been selected for the analysis. This came to 222 firms out of 497 firms, that is around 44 per cent. Out of this, the number of firms which export only is two, those which import only is six, those which export and import is 204, and those which neither export or import is 10. Since the number of purely exporting and purely importing firms was very low, we further classified the exporting and importing firms as net exporters and net importers. By this criterion, we get a sample of 89 as net exporters and 115 firms as net

[12] Kessides (1990) among others.

importers. This constitutes the total sample of firms for testing the relationship between domestic competition and trade performance.

Growth of net exports and net imports is calculated for the regression analysis as the simple average of annual percentage change.

In the case of variables for measuring competition we have already seen that either the SD index or the mobility index can be used along with the speed of adjustment index. We use the mobility index and the speed of adjustment index in the estimation. Mobility index, however, needed some modification. It is not possible to use the Ijiri–Simon index for the present analysis which is at the firm level because IS index[13] by definition is an industry measure since it gives only one observation for each industry (the standard deviation of relative ranks). So, as a proxy for IS index, we use the relative rank of each firm for the initial (1988–9) and terminal period 2000–1 along with the PP index in the regression equation.

The Empirical Results

Table 5.5 shows that net export growth is related to the PP index and the IS index at the 5 per cent and 10 per cent level, respectively. But the explanatory power of the equation is very low. However, it is observed that when an interaction term is introduced, the results are stronger. The explanatory power of the equation has doubled, and at the speed of adjustment, emerges as the important factor influencing export growth. This also tends to validate the Schumpeterian hypothesis of competition in the case of export performance. Thus, the analysis clearly shows that higher the domestic competition, higher the rate of growth of net exports.

As for the relationship between competition and net import growth, Table 5.5 shows that both the speed of adjustment and ISI are related at 5 per cent and 1 per cent level, respectively. But when interaction term is introduced, only ISI is important. There is no improvement in the explanatory power and the interaction term is also not significant. Thus, the analysis clearly shows that while there is a sustained relationship between competition measured in terms of ISI and import growth in the case of speed of adjustment, it is not very consistent.

[13] This is true of the SD index also.

Table 5.5
Domestic Competition and Growth of
Net Exports and Net Import—All Industries

Independent Variable \ Dependent Variable	Net Export Growth		Net Import Growth	
Constant	3.8	−3.7	3.9	5.2
SA	0.87**	15.6*	0.64**	−1.2
IS	−2.6 ***	4.8	−2.8 *	−4.02*
IS* SA	–	−14.6*	–	1.7
$\bar{R}^2$	0.06	0.12	0.13	0.13
DW	2.03	2.02	2.2	2.2
Sample Size	89	89	115	115

Sources: CMIE, Prowess, (2005), GoI [CSO] (1992).
Notes: * significant at 1 per cent, ** at 5 per cent level, *** at 10 per cent level

The finding from the analysis, that is, the significant relationship between competition and growth of imports suggests that with trade liberalization imports have surged. The relevant issue here is to examine whether increased imports have led to increased productivity or a reduction in cost. For this we use a very simple test.[14] What is attempted here is to trace the trend total cost per unit value of output (average cost = AC) for net importing industries. The estimated trend equation is given below.

$$AC = -53.03 + 0.03t \qquad \bar{R}^2 = 0.18$$
$$(-1.9) \qquad (2.3^*)$$

(*significant at 8 per cent level) where AC is average cost.

The result clearly indicates that there is no decline in cost. An analysis of the input structure through input output tables for the two time points, 1989–90 and 1998–9[15] shows that the import intensity of intermediate inputs has increased in the manufacturing sector from 12.8 per cent to 24 per cent over the period. Since this has not been reflected in any cost reduction, increased use of imported intermediates must be for quality improvement.

[14] For related literature and other ways of testing see, Harrison (1994), Levinsohn (1993), Krishna and Mitra (1998), Das and Pant (2006), Balakrishnan et al. (2006).

[15] GoI [CSO] (1997, 2005).

Competition in the post-liberalization period thus seems to have been based on quality difference acquired through imports of intermediates. This could be a probable explanation for the positive relation observed between speed of adjustment and net import growth.

CONCLUSIONS

This chapter clearly shows that domestic competition affects trade performance, the causality running from market structure to trade performance both in relation to growth of net exports and net imports. In the case of exports what seems to come out strongly is the validity of the Schumpeterian theory of innovation since there is a strong relationship between the speed of adjustment of profit rates and export growth. In the case of imports, although it is related to competition, increased imports has not led to reduction in cost. The rising import intensity of intermediates tends to suggest that competition in the post-liberalization period seems to be driven more by quality enhancement/product differentiation.

6

Summary and Conclusions

This book is a theory-informed study of the dynamics of domestic competition in Indian manufacturing industries for the post-liberalization period using a multidimensional approach. The focus is on using dynamic measures of competition for the analysis as they are found more appropriate in the post-liberalization period with its emphasis on growth, improving efficiency, stimulating technical change, and integration with global markets, etc.

The study adapts the widely acknowledged analytical framework for the analysis of the dynamics of competition, and one which has received special attention in recent years, namely the Schumpeterian theory of the capitalist process. This theory stresses the development of new technology, new sources of supply, and new types of organization as the driving force behind competition. Assuming this framework as the underlying basis for inter-firm rivalry, the book tries to uncover the processes behind the competitive behaviour of firms and its implications for structure and performance—the two major dimensions in industrial organization theory. In other words, the analysis broadly falls within the structure, conduct, performance (SCP), paradigm. Of the four core empirical Chapters, Chapters 2 and 3 are devoted to assessing the intensity of competition in terms of the structural indicators—turnover (mobility) of firms and share cutting, respectively. In Chapters 4 and 5, we are concerned with performance indicators—the persistence of profit rates and growth of foreign trade respectively. The entire analysis of the book is based on a balanced sample of 497 firms covering 14 major industries obtained from the CMIE's electronic database, Prowess. Now let us consider the details.

In the literature, the mobility/turnover of firms is identified as one important dimension, a dynamic one, of what constitutes effective competition. At the same time, the mobility index is also not without criticism. The main criticism against it is that it only shows whether the size of a firm is higher or lower than that of another firm but not by how much. Therefore, the lack of stability of the ranks may not capture the extent of competition. The second criticism is that change in the market shares, which is the really significant phenomenon for understanding the market, does not get reflected in the rank analysis. The contention of Chapter 2, titled 'Mobility Analysis: A New Approach' is that if the limitations of the turnover index are taken care of, it can provide several important insights on competition, which cannot be captured by other indicators such as the concentration ratio and is therefore an important tool for public policy. Chapter 2 sets out to provide an alternate turnover index, based on an order preserving transformation of the data and establish that the new index overcomes the limitations of the traditional index. The new index is then used to analyse competition.

Three major exercises are undertaken to get insights into the firms' behaviour and the nature of competition: (i) The stability of size ranks is tested using rank correlation; (ii) The standard deviation of relative ranks for the end points is estimated (Ijiri–Simon method) to understand the change in the degree of competition; and (iii) using transition matrices, an analysis of the change in size structure and mobility patterns is attempted.

Testing for rank shifts in 14 industries at the beginning and end of the period of analysis indicates that 43 per cent of the industries, accounting for 70 per cent of the value added of sample companies, have a rigid size structure suggestive of low competition. It is also observed that mobility improves over the longer period. Analysis of the change in the degree of mobility over the period shows that in six out of 14 industries, the average shifting has come down, suggesting that competition has declined. Out of the remaining eight industries, for one industry (Electrical Machinery), the average shifting remained the same while for the other 50 per cent of industries accounting for 49 per cent of net value added, it has increased. This suggests that only in these seven industries competition has increased. It is also to be noted that the highest average shifting in the initial year was in Metal Products industry (0.051), the lowest was in Cotton Textiles followed by Non-electrical Machinery. In the final year, it was highest again in Metal Products (0.042), but the lowest being Beverage & Tobacco industry followed by Non-electrical Machinery.

The impact of mobility on the size structure is examined by the skewness and kurtosis measures of the distributions. It is observed that in six industries out of 14, that is, about 50 per cent, there is no change in the number of firms in the large size classes. Out of these six industries, three of them (Drugs & Pharmaceuticals, Non-metallic Minerals, and Synthetic Textiles) exhibit change in the identities. In other words, the identity of firms in a class can change even when the frequency does not change. Besides, in these industries, it may be noted, that the concentration ratios could remain the same and yet mobility did occur indicating competition.

The inter- and intra-class mobility of firms is examined for their implication for market structure using transition matrices. The analysis gives the following conclusions. On an average, 55 per cent of the firms remain in the same class, 24 per cent move upward, and 21 per cent downward in the manufacturing sector. Further, the highest percentage of firms remaining in the same class is in the Non-electrical Machinery (86 per cent). The highest upward mobility has occurred in Wood & Paper whereas in the case of downward mobility, it is in Drugs & Pharmaceuticals. Beverages & Tobacco does not show any upward mobility and Non-electrical Machinery indicates very little downward mobility. The study also links up patterns of mobility with market structure. It illustrates the existence of varied types of competition in terms of inter- and intra-class mobility, which cannot be captured by the traditional concentration ratios.

The chapter clearly establishes that the mixing and reordering, upward, and downward mobility of firms in an industry is an important dynamic dimension of what constitutes effective competition. Public policy for increasing competition in the manufacturing sector should give top priority to understanding mobility barriers and suggest ways of eliminating such barriers.

Chapter 3 titled 'Concentration: An Integrated Approach to Static and Dynamic Aspects' is an attempt to understand the vigour of competition in Indian industries using the Grossack model, a model which integrates both static and dynamic measures of concentration—the link between the two being innovation. The main focus of this chapter is to understand the movement of shares among firms by size-class. The essence of Grossack's model is to see: (i) whether large firms of some 'initial' years have been able to maintain their market shares up to some 'terminal' year; and (ii) whether large firms have lost their share to small firms, new entrants, or to other large firms. To capture these requirements, Grossack devises an ingenious decomposition exercise wherein the regression coefficient, obtained by regressing the market shares in the terminal year of the firm on the market share of the initial year, is expressed as a product of the correlation coefficient and the concentration ratio. The parameters of the model are estimated for the short and long periods.

Empirical analysis shows that for all industry groups taken together, there is no change in static concentration between 1988–9 and 1994–5 and a small increase in HI from 0.13 to 0.15 during the period 1994–5 to 2000–1. Comparison over the period 1995 to 2001, aftermath of economic reforms initiated in 1991, shows that Herfindahl index (HI) of concentration in 2001 was higher than in 1995 for 10 industries, lower only in one, and remained the same in three industries. Thus, interestingly it is seen that in the reform period HI increased in a majority of industries. Between 1989 and 1995, such a trend was not noticed. But there are industry variations. Industry-wise analysis shows a high and steady increase in the Herfindahl index in the Beverages and Tobacco industry. As against this, we have Iron and Steel where HI is steadily declining from a high level, implying declining concentration.

Next we analyse the change in the market shares of the industry groups and its components for the short period and the long period for understanding the dynamics of competition and share cutting in Indian industries. From the regression coefficients, we observe the following: in the short period, there are only two industry groups (Beverages and Tobacco and Transport Equipment) which have a value of $b>1$ indicating that the larger firms of the initial year on an average, increased their shares. The increase was 24 per cent and 10 per cent, respectively. A value of $b>1$ is also indicative of increased monopoly power. For the remaining 12 industry groups, the value of b was less than 1. This indicates that larger firms of the initial year, on an average, lost market shares, that is, they could not maintain their shares. In our sample the loss ranged from 10 per cent to 50 per cent. When we move to the long period, it is seen in the Beverages and Tobacco industry that larger firms on an average showed an increase in shares of 38 per cent from the initial year. That is an increase in market shares by 14 per cent, from the middle year. This indicates increasing monopoly power in the long run as well. This, however, was not true in the case of Transport Equipment industry. Although there was monopoly power in this industry in the short run, large firms on average could not maintain market shares in the long run. Instead they lost market shares by 15 per cent. In the short run in the Wood and Paper industry, large firms lost market share on an average (that is, 24 per cent) but in the long run they gained 6 per cent shares from the initial year. This suggests they gained monopoly power over time.

To understand monopoly power and share cutting affecting competition, we adopt Grossack's two-way classification using the value of r (rank correlation) and $\sqrt{C(HI)}$ (square root of the ratio of terminal period Herfindal Index to current), the components of decomposition of the regression coefficient b. Since a value of $b>1$ by itself cannot be considered an indication of monopoly power as noted by Grossack himself, we take high r and high $\sqrt{C(HI)}$, the two components of b, as indicative of the presence of monopoly power. It may be noted that if an industry's r-value is above the mean of all the industries, it is treated as high; otherwise low. In the case of change in concentration ratio, it is high if the value is greater than the average of all industries, otherwise low. By this classification, there are four groups. We grouped the industries accordingly for the short period and the long period. The major findings were as follows. In the short period, there are three industries in Group I (Beverages & Tobacco, Non-metallic Minerals, and Transport Equipment) with monopoly power. The remaining industries where share cutting took place were classified in three groups (Group II, Group III, and Group IV). In Group II, five industries are listed

(Iron & Steel, Metal Products, Non-electrical Machinery, Wood & Paper, and Non-ferrous Metals), where large firms as a group lost shares to small firms. In Group III, in two industries (Drugs and Pharmaceuticals and Electrical machinery), large firms lost shares to other large firms. In Group IV, that is four industries (Food Products, Cotton Textiles, Synthetic Textiles, and Electronics), large firms lost market shares to other large and small firms indicating greater mobility and greater competition.

As for monopoly and share cutting in the long period, there were four industries (Electrical Machinery and Transport Equipment, Wood Paper, and Beverages & Tobacco) falling in the monopoly group (Group I). While Electrical Machinery and Wood & Paper newly joined the group, Non-metallic Minerals, which earlier belonged to this group, lost its monopoly power. Two industries (Transport Equipment and Beverages & Tobacco) continued to maintain or increase their market share both in the short run and long run. At the other extreme in the competitive group, Group IV, the number of industries in the group remained as four both in the short and long run but their composition changed. Cotton Textiles and Electronics continued to remain in the group. Food Products and Synthetic Textiles became less competitive and left the group while Metal Products and Non-ferrous Metals became more competitive and joined the group. Within Group II, the number of industries reduced from five in the short run to two in the long run. They are Iron & Steel and Non-electrical Machinery. In these industries concentration declined as a result of large firms as a group losing their shares to smaller ones. In Group III there was an increase in the number of industries from two in the short run to four in the long run. The four industries are Food Products, Synthetic Textiles, Drugs and Pharmaceuticals, and Non-metallic Minerals. Here concentration declined because large firms lost shares to each other indicative of imperfect/oligopolistic competition. It may be noted that three of them are new entrants.

As a final test of the appropriateness of the methodology on which we have based our conclusions following Grossack, we test for the relationship between the static index of concentration (HI [1989]) and each of the dynamic measures—b, r, and $\sqrt{C(HI)}$ by estimating simple and partial correlation coefficients. We have tested this relationship only for the long period.

The result shows that the static concentration measure is not strongly correlated with the dynamic measures. This reaffirms that monopoly power cannot be assessed in terms of either static or dynamic indicators alone. Only by integrating the two can one assess if monopoly power has changed. The study thus also highlights the importance of the methodology for an accurate assessment of competition.

Although mobility and share cutting have been analysed, the ultimate test of monopoly power depends on the power to maintain high profit rates. It is this which reflects the state of competition. How far firms in our sample have been successful in a competitive environment is the central issue, which needs examination. In the next chapter we therefore move to the analysis of persistence of profits and the speed with which profits converge to the norm.

Chapter 4 titled 'Persistence of Profit Rates' is an attempt to measure competition in Indian industry by analysing profit rates and highlights the need for a dynamic view of competition and its relevance in a fast changing world of innovations, technical change, etc. Using the Schumpeterian theory of capitalist process as the analytical framework, this chapter empirically examines the behaviour of profit rates. According to this view, innovation in products, processes or marketing techniques create temporary monopolistic advantages and excess profits. This attracts imitators and competition will drive these profits back to normal and the process will repeat. In other words, the market is in a flux arising from the allocation of given resources for new products and production techniques and is in disequilibrium at any moment in time. To understand competition in a dynamic dimension, focus is on understanding the persistence of profit rates and the intensity of competition being reflected in the speed with which excess profits get eroded. The chapter empirically tests this proposition using the methodology pioneered by Mueller based on auto-profit equation, commonly used in persistence of profit rates studies. For measuring the strength of competition, Cubbin–Geroski method has been used.

The major findings from this chapter are as follows: A certain proportion of the transitional component of profit rate from the previous year is carried over to the next year. The average proportion carried over is 47 per cent. The average permanent rate of return is estimated to be 9.2 per cent. This is decomposed into the competitive rate and the long-run firm's specific rent. Using Mueller's search procedure, the average competitive rate of profit for manufacturing industries is estimated to be 5 per cent. This gives the average long-run firm specific rent as 4.2 per cent (that is, 9.2 per cent–5 per cent). It is also seen that the observed average profit rate for all industries is 7.5 per cent, which is about 50 per cent higher than the competitive rate. These are the aggregate results.

Inter-industry analysis shows that in four out of the 14 industries (Food Products, Non-ferrous Metals, Non-metallic Minerals, and Drugs & Pharmaceuticals), the observed average profit rate is 100 per cent higher than the competitive rate or even more. The highest percentage of carry over of profits is observed in the Synthetic Textiles, at 56 per cent, and the lowest in Beverages and Tobacco, that is, 34 per cent.

Following Cubbin and Geroski, the strength of competition within and across industries is measured in terms of the time taken for a unit change in the transitory component of profit rate to reduce to its half level. The results show that for all industries on an average it takes 0.9 years. But there are inter-industry variations. Synthetic Textiles took the longest time (1.2 years) and the shortest by Beverages and Tobacco (0.6 years). The chapter also shows that the adjustment coefficient for Indian industries, when compared to the results of Vaidya and Kambhampati, has decreased in the post-liberalization period implying competition has increased in the post-liberalization period.

In Chapter 5 the implications of the Schumpeterian theory for another dimension of performance, namely growth in foreign trade are examined. The Schumpeterian process, through innovation, imitation, etc., creates market imperfections via increasing returns to scale. Helpman and Krugman in their new trade theory emphasized that it is the increasing returns and imperfect competition that dictate trade outcomes. In other words, competitive advantage is emphasized as a major factor that determines trade outcomes rather than comparative advantage. The major prediction of this new trade theory is that domestic market structure is an important determinant of trade performance. Based on these theoretical foundations, the relationship between different measures of competition indicative of domestic market structure, and trade outcomes is tested.

The chapter begins with an assessment of domestic rivalry in 14 industrial groups using the three different methods of measuring domestic competition earlier developed in the book, provides an overview of the trade performance, and moves on to test the relationship between domestic market structure and foreign trade.

Assessing competition by each of the three indicators, 50 per cent of the industries are competitive. However, it was also found that an industry can be competitive in terms of one criterion but need not necessarily be so in terms of others. To identify the most competitive and least competitive industries by all three criteria together, Borda ranking was used. The highest three ranks correspond to the most competitive industries, and the lowest three ranks to the least competitive. The three most competitive industries are Metal Products, Drugs and Pharmaceuticals, and Electronics. The least ones are Cotton Textiles, Non-electrical Machinery, Synthetic Textiles, and Transport Equipment.

An analysis of the trade performance based on the ratios (export intensity, import intensity, net trade, etc.) calculated for the beginning triennium 1988–9 to 1991–2 and ending triennium 1998–9/2000–1, for the 14 industries revealed the following. For all industries, on an average, there was an increase in export intensity, import penetration and trade involvement, and a decrease in the net trade performance ratios. Our analysis shows that although we are still net importers, the NTP index has increased over time from –40% to –13%, suggesting that either our exports have increased or imports declined. Our results show that both export and import intensity has increased, but the former more than the latter. Hence the increase in the NTP index is due to the faster growth of exports.

To test whether domestic competition measured in terms of different indices and trade performances are related, two relationships were tested: (i) between domestic competition and net export growth, and (ii) between domestic competition and net import growth. Based on the correlation between the three indicators of competition developed earlier and the availability of data, two indicators were selected for the regression analysis, Ijiri–Simon Index (ISI) and the speed of adjustment. These relationships are tested for all industries with respect to these two indicators of competition and with and without interaction term. Growth in net exports/net imports between the initial and terminal year was regressed on these two measures of competition. It is important to note that while most studies use only unidimensional index to measure competition, this study uses multidimensional indices. Again they are dynamic measures as against static measures. We would like to emphasize that our specification does not include the standard variables that influence trade performance such as factor endowments, R&D expenditure, product differentiation/advertising intensity, and economies of scale among others, as employed in the extant literature, where, several latent and unmeasurable variables (such as potential threat of entry) are however excluded. In this study the omission of the above-mentioned measurable variables in the specification is taken care of in another way. By using an auto-regression specification, all the above measurable as well as latent variables are implicitly captured in the model. It is important to note that this is because the factors affecting the PP index (speed of adjustment) are identified in the literature as almost the same variables used in the earlier specifications, such as economies of scale, levels of concentration, large capital requirements, and advertising expenditures. Thus, our model specification is more inclusive than the previous models, since it captures both measurable and latent variables.

The analysis shows that net export growth is related to the speed of adjustment and the Ijiri–Simon index at the 5 per cent and 10 per cent levels, respectively. But when an interaction term was introduced, the results were stronger. The explanatory power of the equation had doubled and the speed of adjustment emerged as the important factor influencing export growth. Thus, the analysis clearly showed that higher the domestic competition, higher the rate of growth of exports.

As for the relationship between competition and net import growth, the analysis showed that both the speed of adjustment and ISI were related at 5 per cent and 1 per cent level, respectively. But when the interaction term was introduced, only ISI was important.

There was no improvement in the explanatory power and the interaction term was also insignificant. Thus, the analysis clearly showed that while there was a sustained relationship between competition measured in terms of ISI and import growth, in the case of speed of adjustment it was not very consistent. It may be noted that our results are not consistent with predictions of static measure of competition and foreign trade as theoretically demonstrated by White (1974). His model predicts that market imperfection in the domestic market structure affects imports negatively while its effect on exports is inconclusive. In the present case, the indicators of competition are positively related to export growth while its relationship to import growth is inconclusive. This aspect is further elaborated below.

Now the question is whether increased imports has led to a reduction in cost. This was verified by tracing the trends in total cost per unit value of output (average cost) for net importing industries. From the estimated trend equation of average cost, it was clearly seen that there was no decline in cost. An analysis of the input structure through input-output tables for the two time points, 1989–90 and 1998–9[1], shows that the import intensity of intermediate inputs has increased in the manufacturing sector from 12.8 per cent to 24 per cent over the period. Since this has not been reflected in any cost reduction, increased use of imported intermediates must be for quality improvement. Competition in the post-liberalization period thus seems to have been based on quality difference acquired through imports of intermediates. This could be a probable explanation for the positive relation observed between speed of adjustment and net import growth. More detailed analysis relating to the composition of imports and R&D expenditure, however, are necessary to throw more light on this. This is outside the scope of the present study. We next examine as to how the results of our study compare with those of earlier studies for the Indian manufacturing sector.

A review of the literature clearly shows that different aspects of competition—static, dynamic, and institutional—have been examined for different periods, using different methods and

[1] GOI (1997, 2005).

different databases. We compare our results with the findings of such major studies most pertinent to our analysis.[2]

We begin with static concentration. Kambhampati (1996) showed that there was an increase in concentration (*n*-firm ratio) in 27 per cent of the industries analysed for the period 1974–85. and in 48 per cent of the industries for the period 1983–5. Athreya and Kapur (2006) study for the period, 1978–99, found that the concentration ratio (4-firm) rose in 47 per cent of the industries examined. Ramaswamy (2006) measured changes in market concentration over the period 1993–2002 for 40 selected industry groups in the manufacturing sector using Herfindahl index (HI) and found that in a little over 50 per cent of the industries considered, HI had increased over the period. Bhavani and Bhanumurti (2007) in their analysis found a rise in HI in 38 out of 83 products considered (46 per cent) over the period, 1994–2005. All these studies show that the increase in concentration has ranged from 27 per cent to 50 per cent. If we confine ourselves to the results of the 1990s (Ramaswamy 2006, Bhavani and Bhanumurti 2007). The concentration ranges from 46 per cent to 50 per cent. Our study for the period, 1988–9 to 2000–1, shows that concentration increased in 43 per cent of the industries, which rose to 57 per cent for the period 1995–2001 (see Table 3.1). Our findings are in agreement with those of Ramaswamy and Bhavani et al.

Balakrishnan and Suresh Babu (2003) found that average price cost margins increased in the 1990s in almost all the two digit manufacturing industry groups. Based on the Lerner index of competition, Pant and Pattanayak (2005) conclude that price cost margins were in general high over the 1990s (1989–2003) across all industries, and in most of the industries increasing over the second half of the 1990s (1996–2003). Similarly, Das and Pant's (2006) study for the period 1989–2003 found that competition in the corporate sector had not increased during the post-liberalization period in terms of the difference between price and marginal cost.

[2] More specifically we compare our findings with those of Ramaswamy (2006), Bhavani and Bhanumurti (2007), OECD (2007), Balakrishnan and Suresh Babu (2003), Das and Pant (2006), Athreya and Kapur (2006), Pant and Pattanayak (2005), Vaidya (1993), Kambhampati (1996) and Glen et al. (1999, 2001, 2003) among others.

Thus, one may conclude that most of the studies, based on static indicators, suggest that concentration increased in the manufacturing sector during the post-liberalization period.

How far these findings are reflected in the coefficient of adjustment in profit rates—the dynamic indicator? We examine the following studies by Vaidya (1993), Kambhampati (1995, 1996) and Glen et al. (1999, 2001, and 2003) among others. Vaidya's study (1993), based on balanced sample of 68 firms for the period 1960–87 found that the adjustment coefficients were higher than 0.5 in five sub-samples out of six in India than in advanced countries (0.5 is the upper limit of the coefficient for advanced countries).

Kambhampati's (1995, 1996) studies for the period 1970–85 found that 25 of the 42 industries analysed showed relatively high level of persistence of profit differentials, with adjustment coefficient greater than 0.6, which is greater than our coefficient 0.47. Their period of analysis, however, included only a few years of the early liberalization phase and their results can be taken as reflective of the control regime. Our results for the post-liberalization period 1888–9/2000–1, when compared with those of the above studies, suggest that competition increased consequent to reforms.

Glen et al.'s studies (1999, 2001, and 2003) estimate that the adjustment coefficient is 0.356 for the period 1980–92, 0.221 for the period 1982–92 and 0.213 for the period 1980–95. All these estimates fall below our estimate of 0.47, suggesting lesser competition in the post-liberalization period. The estimates are also far below those of Vaidya and Kambhampati for the pre-liberalization period when controls were very strong. It is quite possible that some of the unexpected results of Glen et al.'s could be due to the choice of the period of analysis and the industries covered. Most of these studies combine the regulatory period and only the initial years of reforms. Our findings on domestic competition and trade performance also support the estimates of Vaidya and Kambhampati instead of Glen et al.

Thus, one can conclude that our study clearly indicates that competition increased in the post-liberalization period as reflected in our adjustment coefficient, which is close to the upper limit of the adjustment coefficient for advanced countries (0.5). Our study clearly brings out the point that competition viewed as an end state (static) and as a process (dynamic) has different implications on the degree of competition.

The working of the institutional framework and its implications for competition has not been gone into in our analysis. This has been taken up by two studies Bhavani and Bhanumurti 2007 and OECD study 2007. We draw on the findings of these studies for some insights on this issue.

Bhavani and Bhanumurti's (2007) study is an assessment of the institutional structures in terms of their adequacy as well as effectiveness in obtaining desired goals of promoting competition. They make a distinction between potential and actual competition in their analysis. Potential competition is studied in relation to the rules and regulations that restrict competition. Important among them are 'general rules and regulations that involve numerous formalities and complex procedures, restrictions, over cross-border trade and foreign direct investment, small industry policies, and labour laws'. The state of actual competition is studied in terms of entry of imports, transnational corporations, and its effects on size distribution, ownership patterns, and forms of business organization over the period 1989–90 and 1997–8.

Their analysis highlights that India ranks 134 out of 175 countries in the survey of 'Doing Business, 2007' by World Bank, thereby suggesting that the rules and regulations of doing business are still complex in India, and the policy induced-entry barriers are one of the highest in the world. In comparative terms, both trade and non-trade barriers are still high and restrict imports as a source of competition. Imports though rising, constitute only less than 1 per cent of the domestic market. India's rank on trade restrictiveness in the international comparison of 91 countries is 13, certainly very high in relative terms. India is still considered an under performer in attracting foreign direct investment and labour regulations inflexible for promoting competition. Thus, the study clearly shows that the institutional framework for increasing competition needs further strengthening.

Another major study on similar lines is the OECD Economic Surveys, India (2007). The analysis is based on OECD's indicators of Product Market Regulation (PMR) in three key areas: state control, barriers to entrepreneurship, and barriers to international trade and investment. PMR indicators are estimated for both overall and specific policies in the three key areas. The study emphasizes the need for further institutional changes focusing on product and input market regulations.

The study found that the overall score[3] (as well as for three sub-components) is much lower than in countries such as Latin America, OECD emerging markets, Euro area, and the United States. In other words, the overall level of product market regulation is still quite high and restricts competition in India. High public ownership in a wide range of products and sectors which are inherently competitive, excessive administrative hurdles for starting a business, restrictive policies relating to trade and investment such as high tariff rates, barriers to firm exit, preference for small-sized firms, limitations of the competition policy (asset limits for mergers, for example), etc., are cited as reasons for this. The study concludes like that of Bhavani and Bhanumurti (2007), that although liberalization had improved the regulatory environment to international best practices in some areas, the overall level of product market regulation in the institutional setup was still restrictive. Thus, the two studies emphasize the need to go further and suggest policy changes if one were to achieve in full, the gains from a competitive environment. The findings of these two studies complement the empirical findings of our study on the state of competition.

To conclude, this study marks a departure from earlier studies both analytically and in terms of methodology. Two overriding concerns in the book are: (i) To emphasize the relevance and appropriateness of viewing competition as a process, most pertinent in the context of liberalization, rather than as an end state of affairs: this is achieved by adopting the Schumpeterian perspective of the capitalist process as the theoretical framework for the study and using dynamic measures to measure competition, (ii) To establish that there are several dimensions to the competitive process and multiple measures are needed to understand the different nuances of it. Towards this end, Chapter two introduces a methodologically improved version of the turnover index—the new turnover index.

[3] The overall score index runs from 0–6, representing the least to the most restrictive regulatory regime.

The new index not only captures economic phenomena such as share changes but also provides better insights on the nature of competition, which static indicators of concentration cannot do. The contribution of Chapter 3 is the application of the Grossack model, which integrates static and dynamics of concentration. Quite in contrast to concentration measures, which estimate the share of different sizes of firms in total output/sales, etc., the new method captures share mobility across sizes of firms. In other words, the model explicitly brings out whether large firms lost shares to other large firms/small firms or to large and small firms etc. This is achieved by integrating static and dynamic aspects of concentration. The findings are also indicative of the different market structures prevailing in different industries. Different market structures reflect different variants of competition and their possible implications for pricing behaviour/profits. While structural and conduct aspects were captured in Chapters 2 and 3, a full picture of the competitive process can be obtained only if we take into account performance aspects. Chapter 4 achieves this by using the Mueller model to estimate the persistence of profit rates. The contribution of this chapter is that it estimates a competitive rate of return and the rent component, which is reflective of the barriers to entry. The final chapter is significant both in analytical and substantive terms. It tests the relationship between domestic competition and foreign trade performance using, dynamic, multidimensional indicators of competition and achieves the integration of industrial organization and trade theories.

Notwithstanding this, the study has some limitations relating to the database. Chapter 2 on mobility analysis required a balanced sample of firms. Since the findings on competition from the different chapters had to be compared, a balanced sample of firms was selected for the entire analysis. This restricted the sample size to 497 firms from 14 somewhat broad industry groups at different levels of aggregation. In addition, we wanted maximum number of firms in each industry for intra-industry analysis, which restricted the data to the year 2000–1. The findings of this study to that extent could be considered tentative. Although our sample of 497 firms is much larger than several other studies, it would be useful to test for the sensitivity of the results using a larger sample of firms and more narrowly defined industries with homogenous output structures. This, however, would depend on the availability of suitable data. In this context, CSO should furnish unit-level data from ASI to researchers in order to facilitate more detailed studies in this area.

POLICY IMPLICATIONS

The findings of this book raise several important policy issues, which we now take up for discussion. One major conclusion from this study is that the intensity of competition increased only in those industries where competition was initially high. This implies that the efforts to stimulate competition have not impacted on all industries uniformly. It is quite possible that sector/industry-specific regulations and overall regulations may be conflicting. This needs to be looked into. This is also reinforced by the overall status of competition in the manufacturing sector, that is, 43 per cent of the industries have a very rigid size structure implying low competition.

The second major point that emerges from the analysis is that 24 per cent of the firms moved upwards while 55 per cent remained in the same class implying that there were mobility barriers. The nature of barriers needs to be identified. It could range from access to inputs or other non-price barriers. While the number of firms in the top size-class has not changed in six out of 14 industries (nearly 50 per cent) in three of them, there are identity changes. Though the identity of the firms has changed in three industries, the control of the market is still in the hands of a few firms, in nearly 50 per cent of the industries implying no change in concentration levels. While the new competition Act does not seek to prevent concentration of market power, the implications of an oligopolistic structure for collusive behaviour, pricing, and hence welfare of the consumers needs to be guarded against. Closely allied to this are the findings of Chapter 3 which show that although overall concentration has only marginally increased, there are inter-industry variations. For instance, it has doubled in Beverages and Tobacco and reduced by 37 per cent in Iron and Steel. It also points out that a wide range of market structures ranging from monopoly to perfect competition exist. To address issues relating to abuse of market power in these industries, different strategies are required. This again stresses the need for industry-specific approaches to policy.

Most importantly, Chapter 4 has some major findings indicating rent-seeking behaviour. It shows that in all industries, on an average, the rate of return for all industries is nearly double that of the estimated competitive return. In other words, the rent component and competitive return are more or less equal. How does this affect consumer welfare? Is there a case for intervention in the interest of social welfare in some industries? It is quite possible that rent (temporary monopolies) can occur when there is improvement in efficiency, new innovations etc. But rent-seeking behaviour across all industries does not seem to signify this. Such issues need detailed examination. To illustrate, in the case of Drugs and Pharmaceuticals (whose rate of return is more than 100 per cent of competitive rate) it is seen that while average cost per unit of output has declined (thanks to competition), it has not been transmitted to the consumer as the rising drug prices indicate. This anomaly needs to be addressed in the interests of consumers. Are domestic mergers in the drug industry responsible for this? Or is it the recent decontrol of drug prices that has led to this? This brings into focus the question of weighing whether a separate regulatory authority, a sector-wise policy, or a general competition policy will be more effective.

Chapter 5 shows that by the most stringent test, three industries, namely Drugs and Pharmaceuticals, Electronics, and Metal Products are the only competitive industries (that is, 21 per cent) in the manufacturing sector. The sources of success of the competitive industries deserve further study for the lessons that they could offer. At the other end of the spectrum we have the four least competitive industries—Cotton Textiles, Non-electrical Machinery, Synthetic Textiles, and Transport Equipment. What ails these industries needs to be looked into. Are there still redundant policies in the current framework, which disallow exit, and prop sick units? More investigations are necessary to establish the reasons for this phenomenon.

It is also seen that higher the domestic competition, better the export performance. Domestic competition is also related to imports but this has not led to decrease in cost. This could be due to the quantum and nature of imports or inadequate R&D effort. Other studies also show that institutional factors were not favourable (Bhavani and Bhanumurti 2007). This calls for a more detailed review of import and tariff structure, determinants of R&D, and a change in institutional factors that facilitate competition.

Besides the various issues cited above, this book raises two major areas of future research:

(i) The impact of product market deregulation on employment and related issues, and
(ii) The empirical verification of the Schumpeterian theory of the capitalist process of growth continues to remain a challenge and needs to be resolved.

To sum up, the book raises several issues. While we have found answers for some, there are others for which we have yet to find answers. It therefore leaves something clearly for the future.

References

Athreya, S. and S. Kapur (2006), 'Industrial Concentration in a Liberalizing Economy: A Study of Indian Manufacturing', *Journal of Development Studies*, Vol. 42, No. 6, pp. 981–99.

Ahluwalia, I.J. (1985), *Industrial Growth in India: Stagnation since the Mid-sixties*, Oxford University Press, Delhi.

Balakrishnan, P., M. Parameswaran, K. Pushpangadan, and Suresh M. Babu (2006), 'Liberalization, Market Power and Productivity Growth in Indian Industry', *The Journal of Policy Reform,* Vol. 9, No. 1, pp. 55–73.

Balakrishnan, P. and Suresh M. Babu (2003), 'Growth and Distribution in Indian Industry in the Nineties', *Economic and Political Weekly*, September, Vol. 38, No. 20–6, pp. 3997–4005.

Baldwin, J.R. (1998), *The Dynamics of Industrial Competition: A North American Perspective*, Cambridge University Press, Cambridge.

Basant, R. and S. Morris (2000), 'Competition Policy in India: Issues for a Globalizing Economy', *Economic and Political Weekly,* Vol. 35, No. 31, pp. 2735–47.

Baskar, M.V. (1992), 'Concentration in Indian Manufacturing Industry: 1970 to 1990', Centre for Development Studies, Trivandrum.

Basu, K. (1993), *Lecture in Industrial Organization Theory*, Blackwell Publishers, Oxford, UK.

Baumol, W.J. (2002), *Free Market Innovation Machine*, Princeton University Press, Princeton.

Bhaduri, A. (2007), *Growth, Distribution, and Innovations: Understanding their Interrelations*, Routledge, London.

Bhagwati, J. (1993), *India in Transition, Freeying the Economy*, Clarendon Press, Oxford.

Bhagwati, J. and P. Desai (1970), *India: Planning for Industrialization*, Oxford University Press, New Delhi.

Bhagwati, J. and T.N. Srinivasan (1993), 'India's Economic Reforms', paper prepared by the Ministry of Finance, Government of India.

Bhattacharjea, A. (2001), 'Competition Policy: India and the WTO,' *Economic and Political Weekly*, Vol. 36, No. 51, pp. 4710–13.

Bhavani, T.A. and N.R. Bhanumurti (2007), 'The State of Competition in the Indian Manufacturing Sector', Institute of Economic Growth and Competition Commission of India, New Delhi.

Blaug, M. (1997), 'Competition as an End-State and Competition as a Process', in Curtis Eaton, B., Richard, G., Harris. (eds), *Trade Technology and Economics*, Edward Elgar, UK.

Boyle, S.E. and R.L. Sorenson (1971), 'Concentration and Mobility: Alternative Measures of Industrial Structure', *The Journal of Industrial Economics*, Vol. 19, No. 2, pp. 118–32.

Chakravarty, S. (1987), *Development Planning: The Indian Experience*, Clarendon Press, Oxford.

Choudhury, M. (2002), 'Potential Selectivity Bias in Data: An Evaluation of a Firm–level Database on Indian Industry', *Economic and Political Weekly*, Vol. 37, No. 8, pp. 758–66.

Clark, J.M. (1940), 'Toward a Concept of Workable Competition', *American Economic Review*, Vol. 30, pp. 241–56.

________ (1961), *Competition as a Dynamic Process*, Brookings Institution, Washington.

CMIE, (1997), Prowess (Electronic Data), Mumbai.

________ (1997a), Prowess Users' Manual, Vol. 1, Mumbai.

________ (2001), Prowess (Electronic Data), Mumbai.

________ (2005), Prowess, Mumbai.

Cubbin, J.S. and P.A. Geroski (1990), 'The Persistence of Profits in the United Kingdom', in: Mueller, D.C. (ed.), *The Dynamics of Company Profits: An International Comparison*, Cambridge University Press, New York.

Curry, B. and K.D. George (1983), 'Industrial Concentration: A Survey', *The Journal of Industrial Economics*, Vol. 31, No. 3, pp. 203–55.

Das, S.K. and M. Pant (2006), 'Measuring Market Imperfections in the Manufacturing Sector: Theory and Evidence from India', *Journal of International Trade and Economic Development*, Vol. 15, No. 1, pp. 63–71.

Demsetz, H. (1982), *Economic, Legal and Political Dimensions of Competition*, North Holland Publisher, Amsterdam.

Downie, J. (1958), *The Competitive Process*, Gerald Duckworth, London.

Enders, Walter (2004), *Applied Econometric Time Series*, 2nd edition, John Wiley & Sons, Inc., USA.

Freeman, Chris (2003), 'A Schumpeterian Renaissance', Electronic Working Paper Series, No. 12, The Freeman Centre, University of Sussex, UK.

Geroski, P.A. and A. Jacquemin (1988), 'The Persistence of Profits: A European Comparison', *The Economic Journal,* Vol. 98, No. 391, pp. 375–89.

Geroski, P.A. (1990), 'Modeling Persistent Profitability', in: Mueller, D.C. (ed.), *The Dynamics of Company Profits: An International Comparison*, Cambridge University Press, New York.

Geroski, P.A. and D.C. Mueller (1990), 'The Persistence of Profits in Perspective', in Mueller, D.C. (ed.), *The Dynamics of Company Profits: An International Comparison*, Cambridge University Press, New York.

Glen, J., K. Lee, and A. Singh (2003), 'Corporate Profitability and the Dynamics of Competition in Emerging Markets: A Time Series Analysis', *The Economic Journal,* Vol. 113, pp. F465–84.

________ (2001), 'Persistence of Profitability and Competition in Emerging Markets', *Economic Letters,* Vol. 72, pp. 247–53.

Glen, J., A. Singh, and R. Matthias (1999), 'How Intensive is Competition in the Emerging Markets: An Analysis of Corporate Rates of Return from Nine Emerging Markets', IMF Working Paper 99/32, Washington, D.C., USA.

Gort, M. (1963), 'Analysis of Stability and Change in Market Shares', *Journal of Political Economy*, Vol. 71, No. 1, pp. 51–63.

Government of India, [GoI] (1964), Report of the Committee on Distribution of Income and Levels of Living, Planning Commission, New Delhi.

________ (1965), Report of the Monopolies Inquiry Commission, (Chairman K.C. Das Gupta), Vol. 1 & 2, Ministry of Finance, New Delhi.

________ (1967), *Report on Industrial Planning and Licencing Policy,* headed by R.K. Hazari, Planning Commission, New Delhi.

________ (1969), *Report of the Industrial Licencing Policy Inquiry Committee*, headed by S. Dutt, Ministry of Industrial Development, Internal Trade and Company Affairs, New Delhi.

________ (1978), *Report of the Committee on Imports–Exports Policies and Procedures*, headed by P.C. Alexander, Ministry of Commerce, New Delhi.

________ (1979), *Report of the Committee on Controls and Subsidies*, headed by V. Dagli, Ministry of Finance, New Delhi.

________ (1980), *Committee on Export Strategy: 1980s,* headed by P. Tandon, Final Report, Ministry of Commerce, New Delhi.

________ (1980), *Report of the National Transport Policy Committee*, headed by B.D. Pande, Planning Commission, New Delhi.

________ (1980), *Report of the Committee on Power*, headed by V.G. Rajadhyaksha, Ministry of Energy and Coal, New Delhi.

Government of India (1986), Report of the Committee to examine Principles of Possible Shift from Physical to Financial Controls, Ministry of Finance, New Delhi. (M. Narasimham)

________ (1992), Annual Survey of Industries, Summary Results for the Factory Sector 1988–9, Central Statistical Organization [CSO], Ministry of Planning and Programme Implementation, New Delhi.

________ (1997), Input–Output Transactions Tables 1989–90, Central Statistical Organization [CSO], Ministry of Planning and Programme Implementation, New Delhi.

________ (2000), *Report of the High Level Committee on Competition Policy Law*, Planning Commission, New Delhi.

________ (2003), *The Competition Act 2002*, Ministry of Law and Justice, The Gazette of India, New Delhi.

________ (2005), Input–Output Transactions Tables 1989–99, Central Statistical Organization [CSO], Ministry of Planning and Programme Implementation, New Delhi.

________ (2007), *Report of the Working Group on Competition Policy*, Planning Commission, New Delhi.

Grossack, I.M. (1965), 'Towards an Integration of Static and Dynamic Measures of Industrial Concentration', *Review of Economics and Statistics*, Vol. 47, No. 3, pp. 301–8.

Harrison, A.E. (1994), 'Productivity, Imperfect Competition and Trade Reforms; Theory and Evidence', *Journal of Industrial Economics*, Vol. 36, pp. 53–73.

Hart, P.E. and S.J. Prais (1956), 'The Analysis of Business Concentration: A Statistical Approach', *Journal of the Royal Statistical Society*, Series A, Vol. 119, Pt. 2, pp. 150–81.

Hayek, F.A. (1948), 'The Meaning of Competition', in F.A. Hayek (ed.), *Individualism and Economic Order*, George Routledge & Sons, London, pp. 92–107.

Hazari, R.K. (1966), *The Structure of the Corporate Private Sector: A Study of Concentration, Ownership, and Control*, Asia Publishing School, Bombay.

Helpman, E. and P.R. Krugman (1985), *Market Structure and Foreign Trade: Increasing Returns, Imperfect Competition, and the International Economy*, MIT Press, Cambridge.

________ (1989), *Trade Policy and Market Structure*, MIT Press, Cambridge.

Hymer, S. and P. Pashigian (1962), 'Turnover of Firms as a Measure of Market Behaviour', *The Review of Economics and Statistics*, Vol. XLIV, No. 1, pp. 82–7.

Ijiri, Y. and H.A. Simon (1977), *Skewed Distributions and the Size of Business Firms*, North Holland Publishing Co., Amsterdam.

Joskow, J. (1960), 'Structural Indicia: Rank–Shift Analysis as a Supplement to Concentration Ratios', *The Review of Economics and Statistics*, Vol. XLII, pp. 113–16.

Kambhampati, U.S. (1995), 'The Persistence of Profit Differentials in Indian Industry', *Applied Economics*, Vol. 27, pp. 353–61.

________ (1996), *Industrial Concentration and Performance*, Oxford University Press, Mumbai.

Kessides, I.N. (1990), 'The Persistence of Profits in U.S. Manufacturing Industries', in Mueller D.C. (ed.), *The Dynamics of Company Profits, An International Comparison*, Cambridge University Press, New York.

Kirzner, I.M. (1973), *Competition and Entrepreneurship*, University of Chicago Press, Chicago.

Kmenta, J. (1971), *Elements of Econometrics*, Macmillan, New York.

Krishna, P. and D. Mitra (1998), 'Trade Liberalisation, Market Discipline and Productivity Growth: New Evidence from India', *Journal of Development Economics*, Vol. 56, No. 2, pp. 447–62.

Krugman, Paul, R. (1994), *Rethinking International Trade*, MIT Press, Cambridge.

________ (1996), 'Making Sense of the Competitiveness Debate', *The Oxford Review of Economic Policy*, Vol. 12, No. 3, pp. 17–25.

Lall, S. (2001), 'Competitiveness Indices and Developing Countries: An Economic Evaluation of the Global Competitiveness Report', *World Development*, Vol. 29, No. 9, pp. 1501–25.

Levinsohn, J. (1993), 'Testing the Imports as Market Discipline Hypothesis', *Journal of International Economics*, Vol. 35, pp. 1–22.

Mehta, P.S. (2006), (ed.) *A Functional Competition Policy for India*, CUTS International, Jaipur.

________ (2007), (ed.) *Competition and Regulation in India*, CUTS International, Jaipur.

McNulty, P.J. (1967), 'A Note on the History of Perfect Competition', *Journal of Political Economy*, Part1, Vol. 75, No. 4, pp. 395–7.

________ (1968), 'Economic Theory and the Meaning of Competition', *Quarterly Journal of Economics*, Vol. 82, No. 4, pp. 639–56.

Mueller, D.C. (1977), 'The Persistence of Profits above the Norm', *Economica*, Vol. 44, pp. 369–80.

________ (1986), *Profits in the Long Run*, Cambridge University Press, Cambridge.

________ (1990), (ed.), *The Dynamics of Company Profits, An International Comparison*, Cambridge University Press, New York.

Nelson, Richard, R., and Sidney, G. Winter (1982), *An Evolutionary Theory of Economic Change*, MA: Harward University Press, Cambridge.

Nolle, Daniel, E. (1991), 'An Empirical Analysis of Market Structure and Import and Export Performance for US. Manufacturing Industries', *Quarterly Review of Economics and Business*, Vol. 31, No. 4, pp. 59–78.

Odagiri, H., H. Yamawaki (1990), 'The Persistence of Profits in Japan', in: Mueller, D.C. (ed.), *The Dynamics of Company Profits: An International Comparison*, Cambridge University Press, Cambridge, pp. 169–85.

OECD (2007), Economic Surveys India, Vol. 14, OECD, Paris.

Pagoulatos, E. and R. Sorensen (1976), 'Domestic Market Structure and International Trade: An Empirical Analysis', *Quarterly Review of Economics and Business*, Vol. 16, No. 1, pp. 45–59.

Panagariya, A. (2008), *India: The Emerging Giant*, Oxford University Press, New York.

Pant, M. and M. Pattanayak (2005), 'Does Openness Promote Competition? A Case Study of Indian Manufacturing', *Economic and Political Weekly*, Vol. 40, No. 39, pp. 4226–31.

Patterson, K. (2000), *An Introduction to Applied Econometrics, A Time Series Approach*, Macmillan Press Ltd, London.

Penrose, E. (1980), *The Theory of the Growth of the Firm*, 2nd edition, Basil Blackwell, Oxford.

Pickering, J.F. and I.M. Sheldon (1984), 'International Trade Performance and Concentration in British Industries', *Applied Economics*, Vol. 16, pp. 421–42.

Porter, M.E. (1990), *The Competitive Advantage of Nations*, Free Press, New York.

________ (1998), *On Competition*, Harward Business School Press, Boston.

Pugel, A. Thomas (1980), 'Foreign Trade and US Market Performance', *The Journal of Industrial Economics*, Vol. 29, No. 2, pp. 119–29.

Pushpangadan, K. and N. Shanta (2004), 'Concentration and Market Structure: A Case Study of Dominant Firms with Fringe Competition in Indian Industry', *The ICFAI Journal of Industrial Economics*, Vol. 1, No. 1, pp. 7–19.

________ (2005), 'Competition in Indian Manufacturing Industries: A Study using Static and Dynamic Measures of Concentration', *The ICFAI Journal of Industrial Economics*, Vol. 2, No. 1, pp. 34–40.

________ (2006), 'Competition in Indian Manufacturing Industries—A Mobility Analysis', *Economic and Political Weekly*, Vol. XLI, No. 39, pp. 4130–9.

Qizil Bash, M. (2002), 'A Note on the Measurement of Poverty and Vulnerability in the South African Context', *Journal of International Development*, Vol. 14, pp. 757–72.

Ramaswamy, K.V. (2006), 'State of Competition in the Indian Manufacturing Industry', in Pradeep S. Mehta (ed.), *A Functional Competition Policy for India*, CUTS International, Jaipur and Academic Foundation, Delhi, pp. 155–64.

Sakakibara, M. and M.E. Porter (2001), 'Competing at Home to Win Abroad: Evidence from Japanese Industry', *The Review of Economics and Statistics*, Vol. 83, No. 2, pp. 310–22.

Samuelson, P. and W.D. Nordhaus (1992), *Economics*, 14th edition, McGraw-Hill, New York.

Scherer, F.M. (1973), *Industrial Market Structure and Economic Performance*, Rand McNally and Co., Chicago.

Schumpeter, Joseph A. (1934), *The Theory of Economic Development*, Harvard University Press, Cambridge.

________ (1950), *Capitalism, Socialism, and Democracy*, 3rd edition, Harper and Row, New York.

Shalit, S. and U. Sankar (1977), 'The Measurement of Firm Size', *Review of Economics and Statistics*, Vol. LIX, No. 3, pp. 290–8.

Shanta, N. and Dennis Raja Kumar (1999), 'Corporate Statistics: The Missing Numbers', *Journal of Indian School of Political Economy*, Vol. 11, No. 4.

Shepherd, W.G. (1982), 'Causes of Increased Competition in the U.S. Economy 1939–1980', *Review of Economics and Statistics*, Vol. LXIV, pp. 613–26.

Simon, H.A. and C.P. Bonini (1958), 'The Size Distribution of Business Firms', *American Economic Review*, Vol. XLVIII, pp. 607–17.

Singh, A. and G. Whittington (1968), *Growth, Profitability, and Valuation*, Cambridge University Press, London.

Sloman, J. (1994), *Economics*, 2nd edition, Harvester Whestsheaf, Hemel Hempstead, UK. W.W. Norton, New York.

Srinivasan, T.N. (2000), *Eight Lectures on India's Economic Reforms*, Oxford University Press, New Delhi.

Stigler, G.J. (1957), 'Perfect Competition: Historically Contemplated', *Journal of Political Economy*, Vol. LXV, No. 1, pp. 1–17.

________ (1963), *Capital and Rates of Return in Manufacturing Industries*, Princeton University Press, New Jersey.

________ (1987), 'Competition', in J. Eatwell, M. Milgate, and P. Newman, (eds), *The New Palgrave*, MacMillan, London, pp. 531–5.

Stiglitz, J.E. (1993), *Economics* W.W. Norton, New York.

Sutton, J. (1997), 'Gibrat's Legacy', *Journal of Economic Literature*, Vol. XXXV, pp. 40–59.

Vaidya, R. (1993), 'The Persistence of Profits: The Indian Experience', *Journal of Quantitative Economics*, Vol. 9, No. 2, pp. 333–48.

Veeramani, C. (2001), 'Analysing Trade Flows and Industrial Structure of India: The Question of Data Harmonization', Working Paper Series, No. 321, Centre for Development Studies, Trivandrum, November.

Vickers, J. (1995), 'Concepts of Competition', *Oxford Economic Papers*, Vol. 47, No. 1, pp. 1–23.

Virmani, A (2006), 'The Dynamics of Competition: Phasing of Domestic and External Liberalisation in India', Working Paper No. 4/2006, Planning Commission, New Delhi.

White, Lawrence, J. (1974), 'Industrial Organisation and International Trade: Some Theoretical Considerations', *The American Economic Review*, Vol. 64, No. 6, pp. 1013–20.

Yamawaki, H., and B.A. David (1988), 'Import Share Under international Oligopoly with Differentiated Products: Japanese Imports in US Manufacturing', *The Review of Economics and Statistics* Vol. 70, No. 4, pp. 569–79.

Yule, Kendall, M.G. (1965), *Introduction to the Theory of Statistics*, Charles Griffin, London.

Yurtoglu, B. Burcin (2004), 'Persistence of Firm–level Profitability in Turkey', *Applied Economics*, Vol. 36, pp. 615–25.

Index